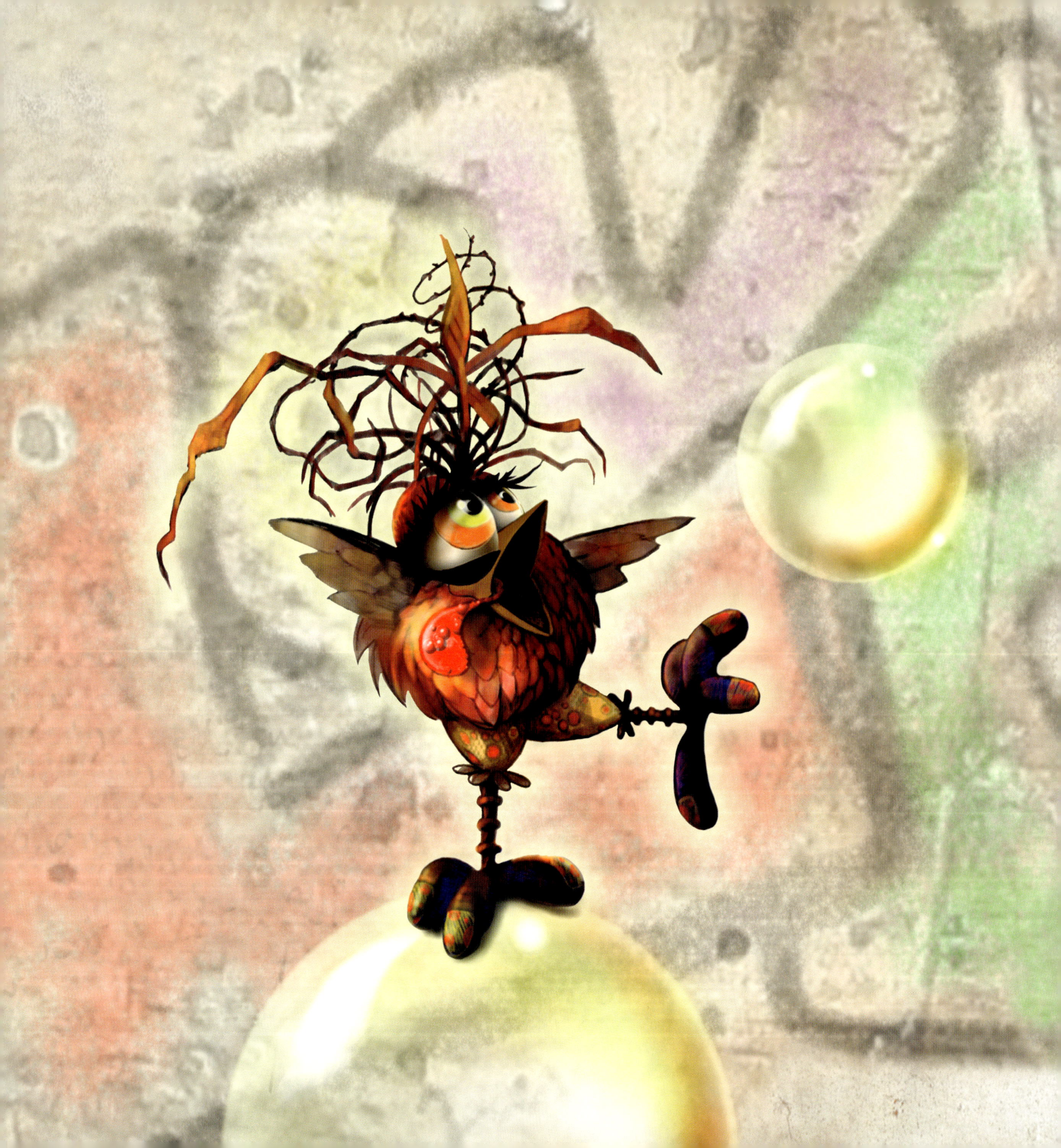

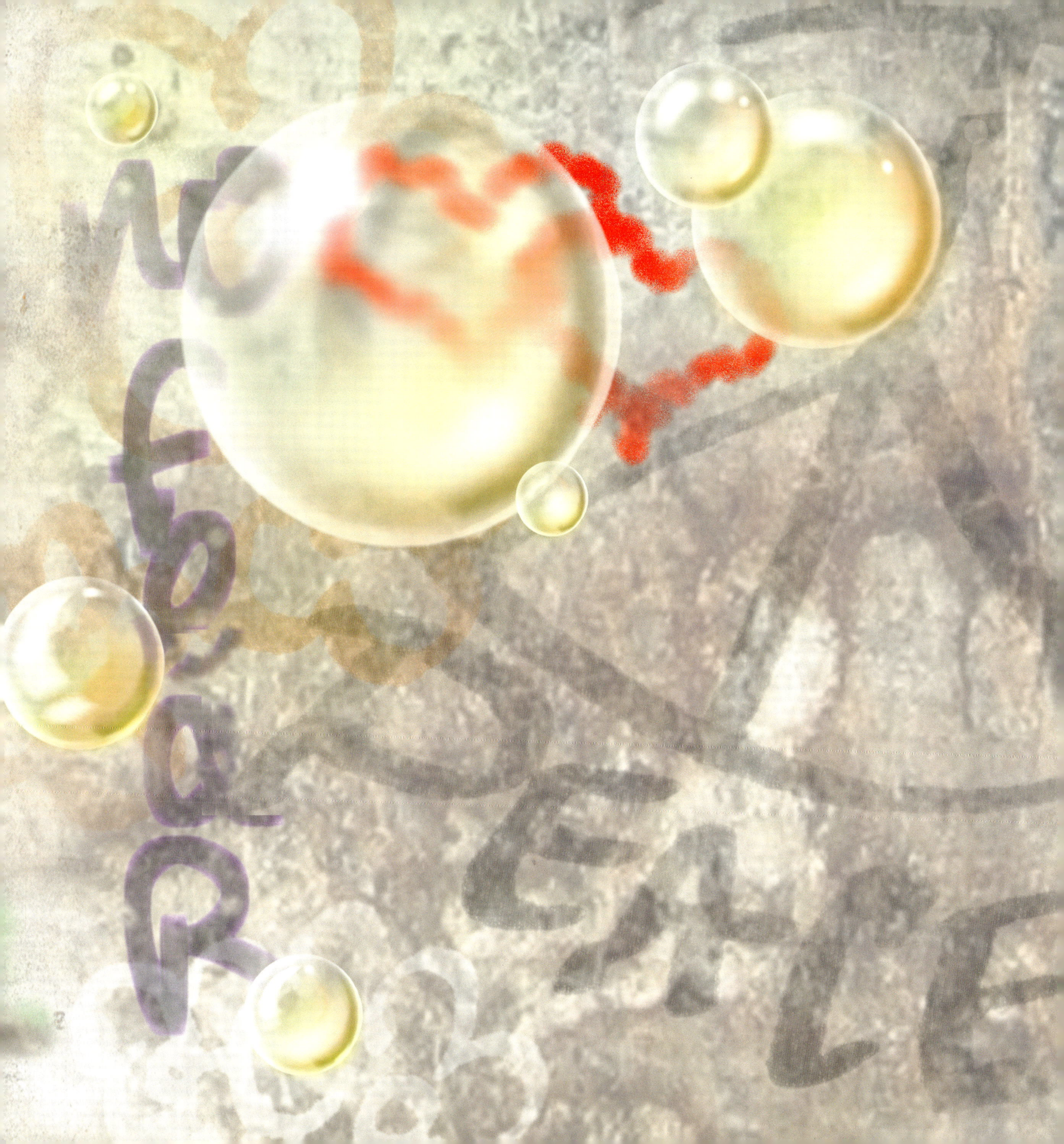

TO:

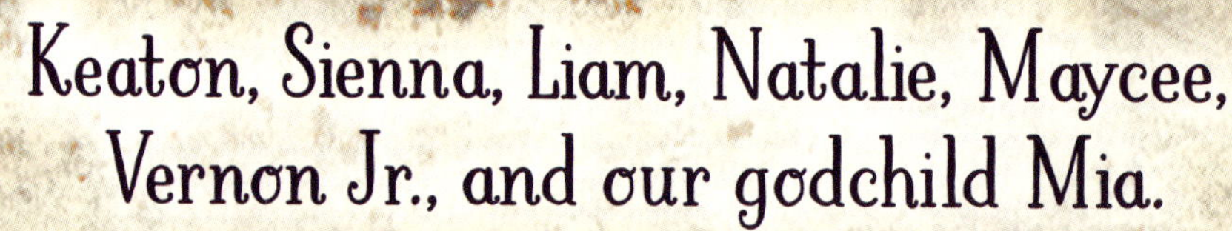

Keaton, Sienna, Liam, Natalie, Maycee,
Vernon Jr., and our godchild Mia.

May you never lose your sense of adventure
and wonderment.

PAPA & NANA

This silly book is a reminder that each of
you (Birds) are unique. There is not another
Bird quite like you.
You are here on purpose, for a purpose...one
of a kind...the perfect YOU.
Remember, you already have wings...

BE THE BIRD!

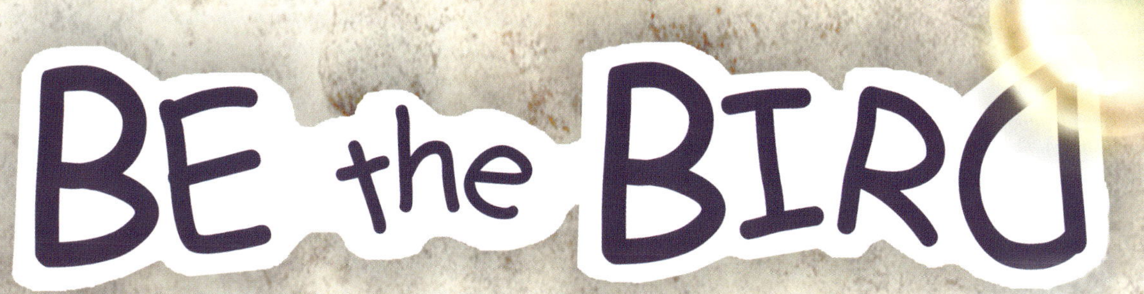


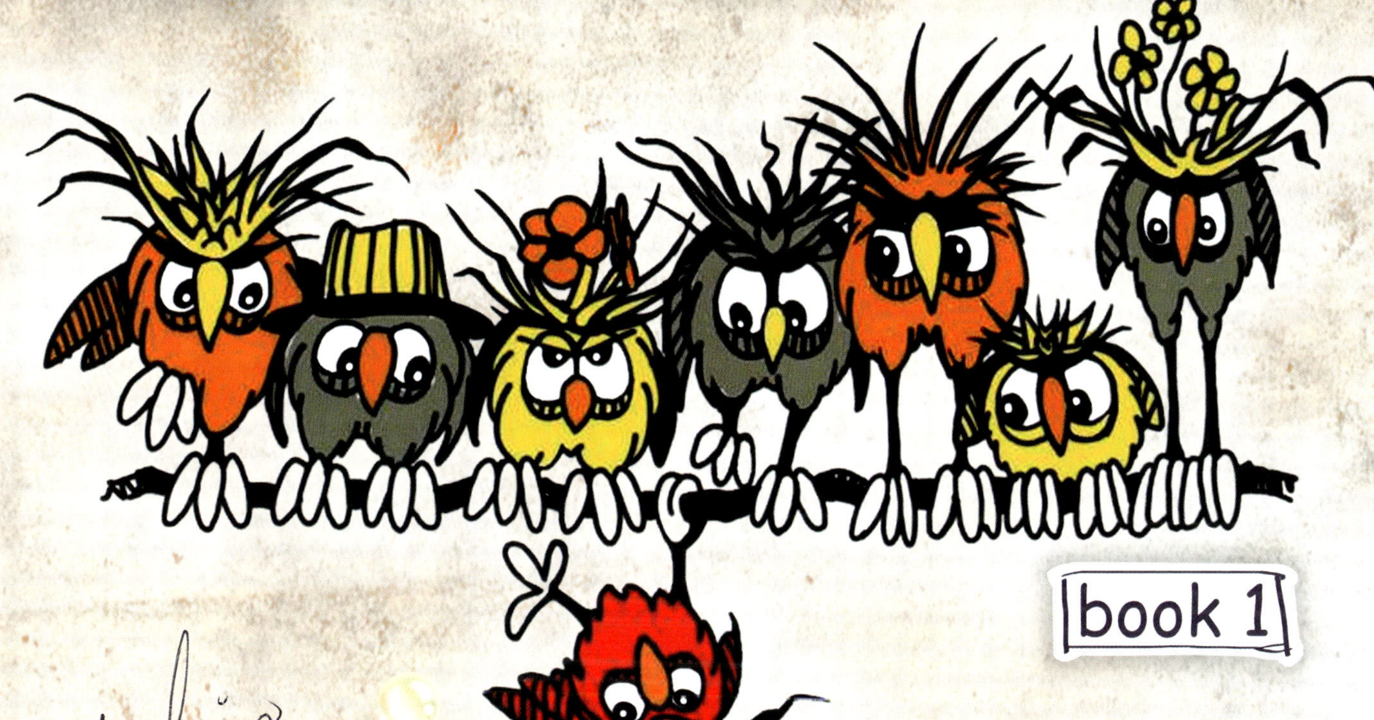

book 1

Richard Lorenz

&

Tina Louise

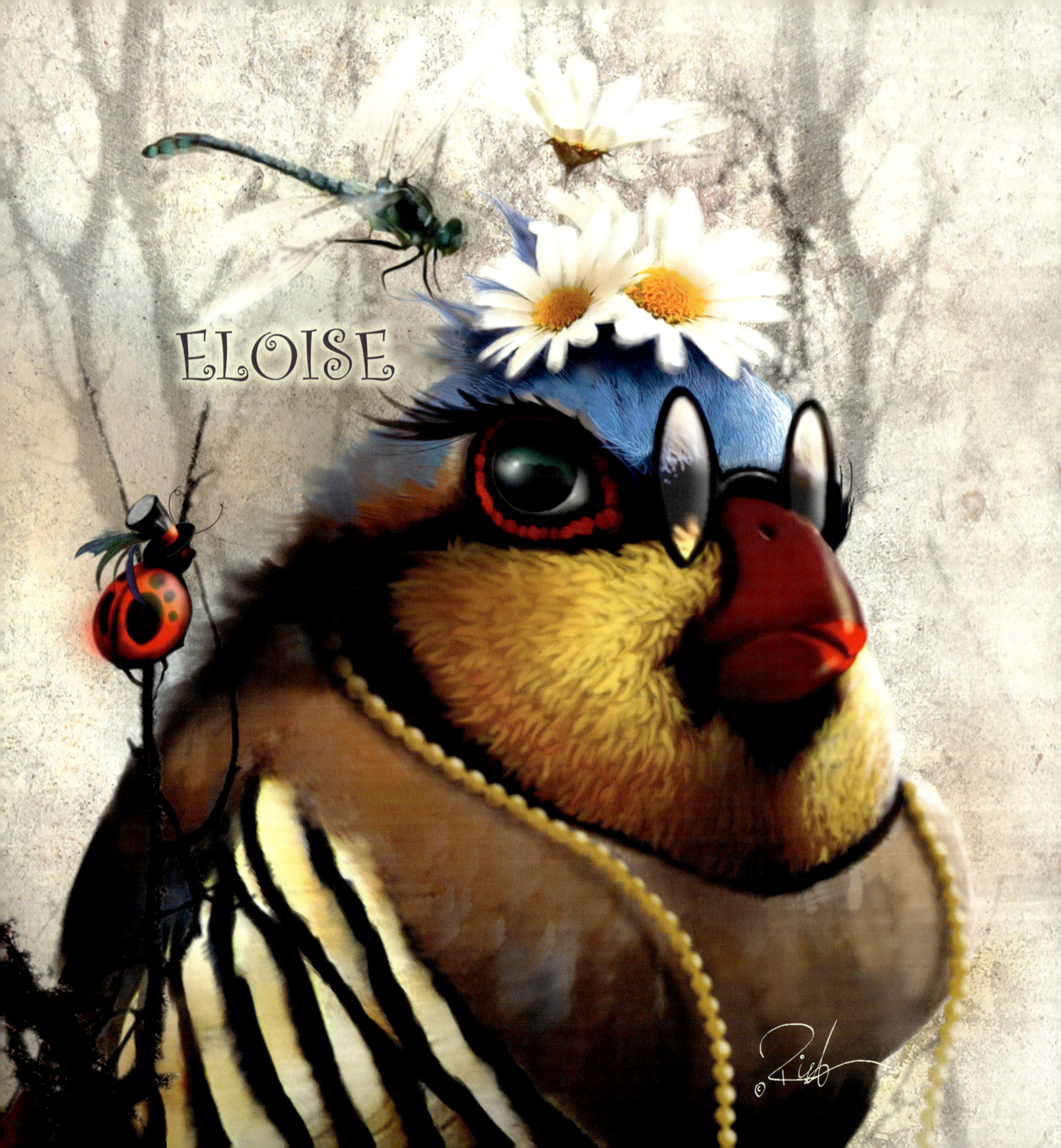
ELOISE

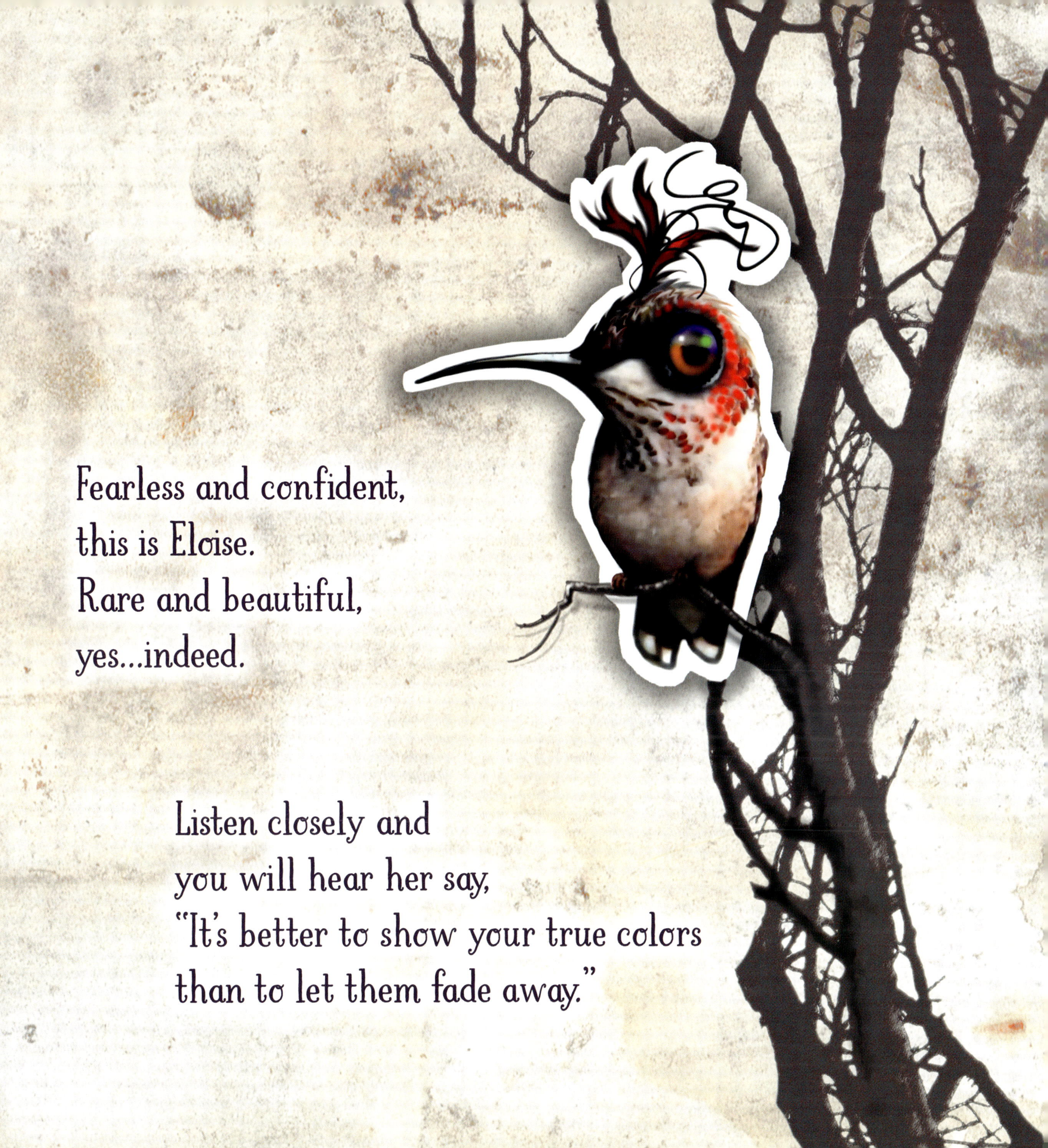

Fearless and confident,
this is Eloise.
Rare and beautiful,
yes...indeed.

Listen closely and
you will hear her say,
"It's better to show your true colors
than to let them fade away."

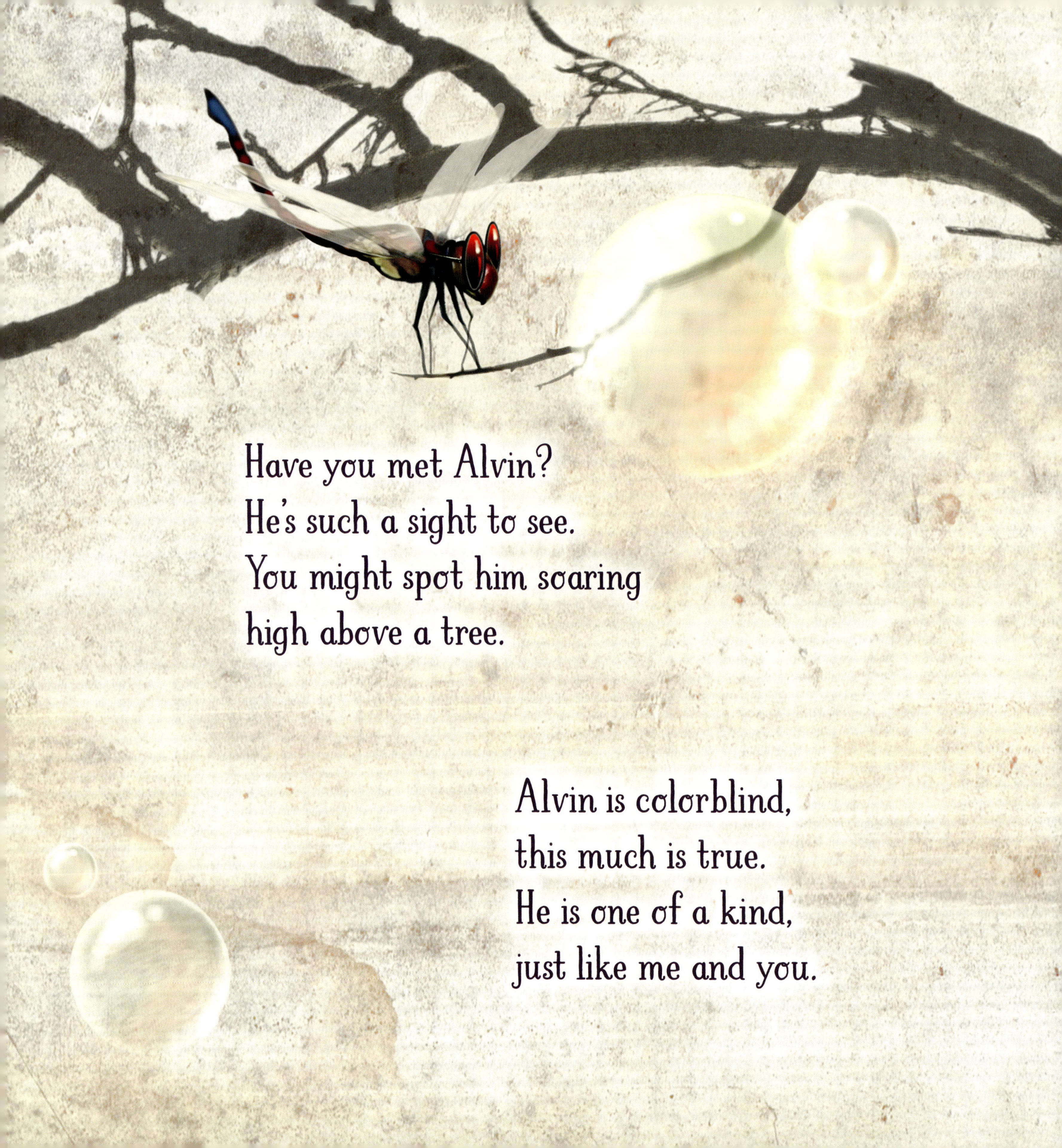

Have you met Alvin?
He's such a sight to see.
You might spot him soaring
high above a tree.

Alvin is colorblind,
this much is true.
He is one of a kind,
just like me and you.

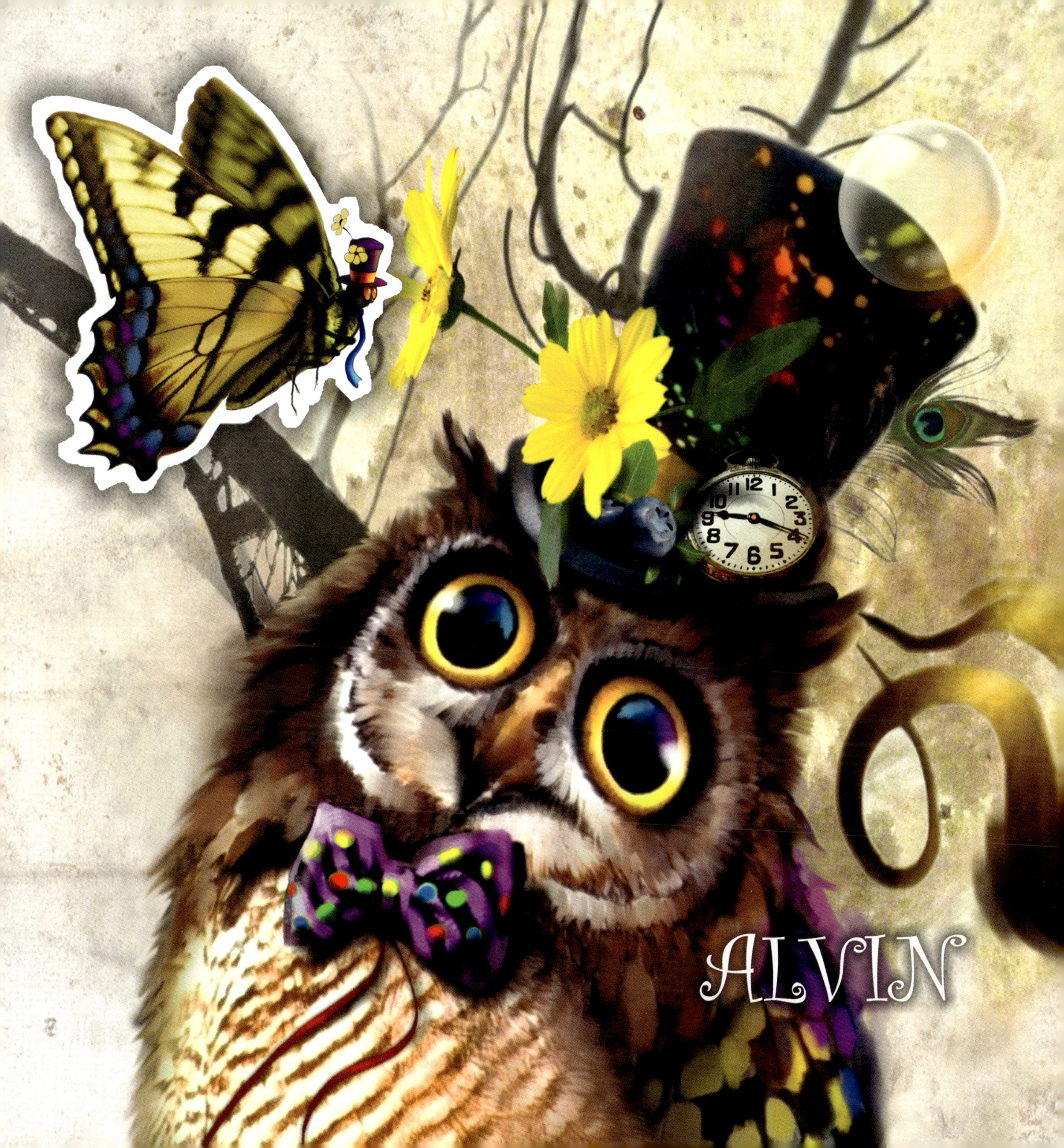
ALVIN

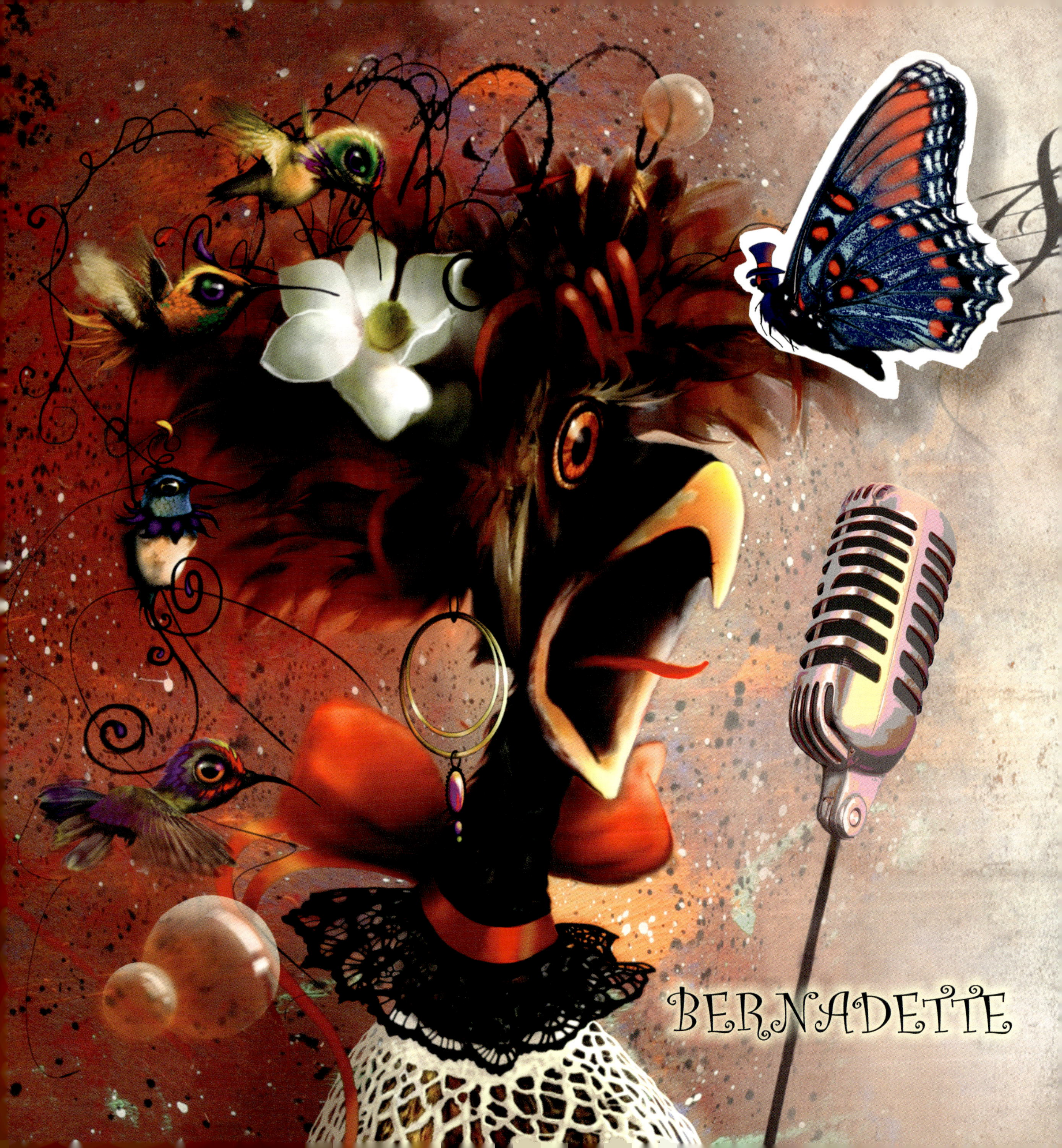
BERNADETTE

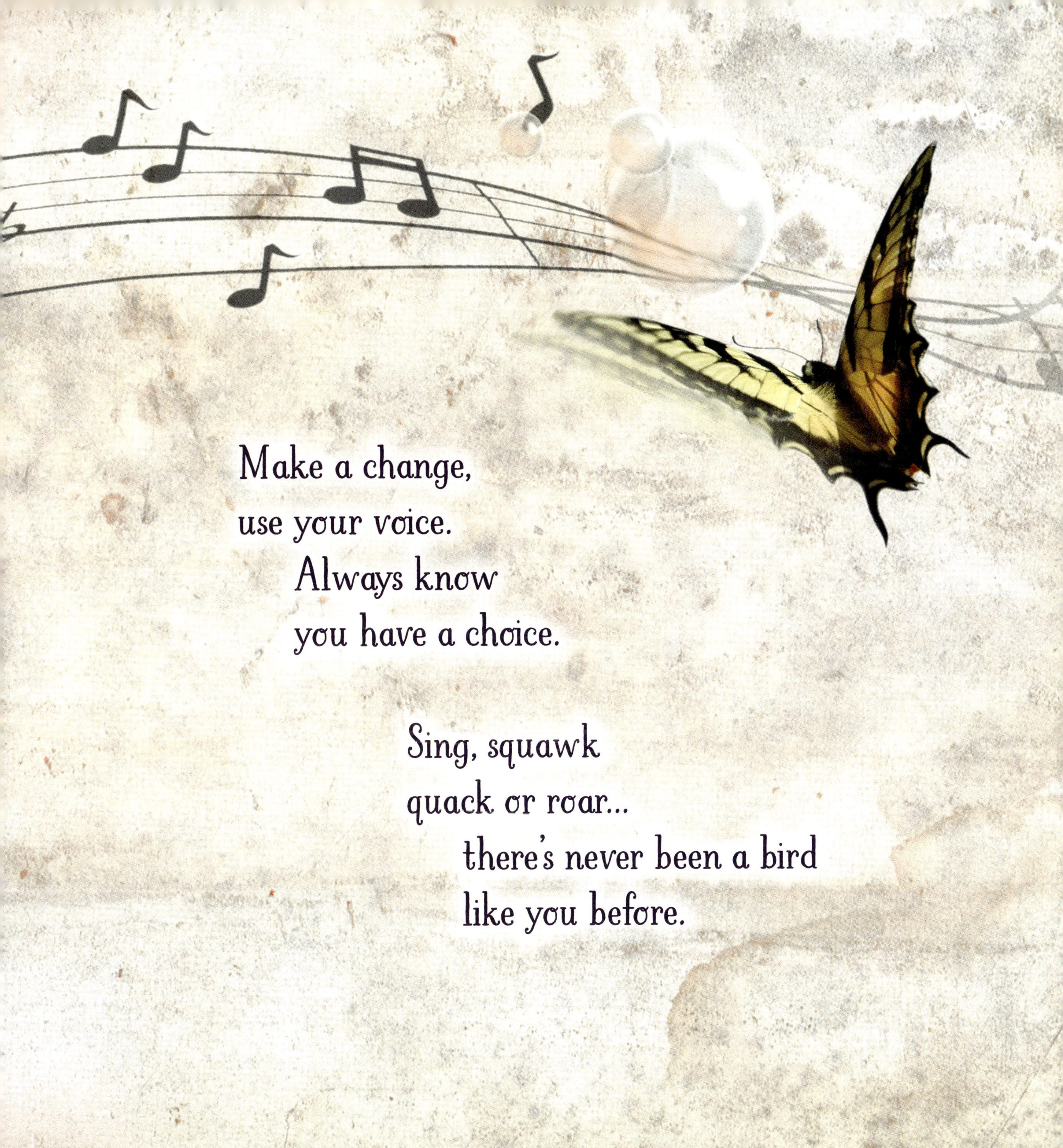

Make a change,
use your voice.
Always know
you have a choice.

Sing, squawk
quack or roar...
there's never been a bird
like you before.

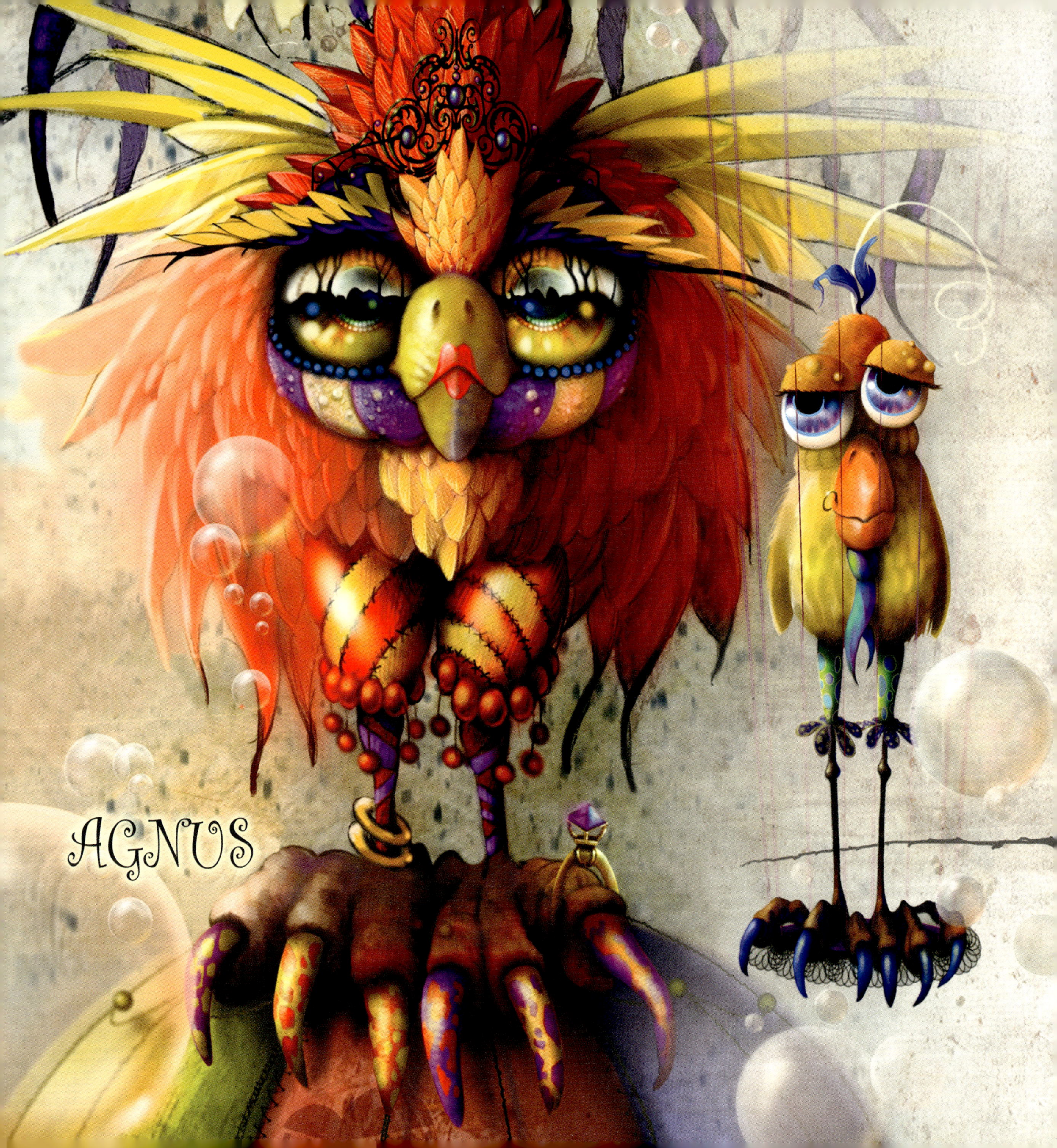
AGNUS

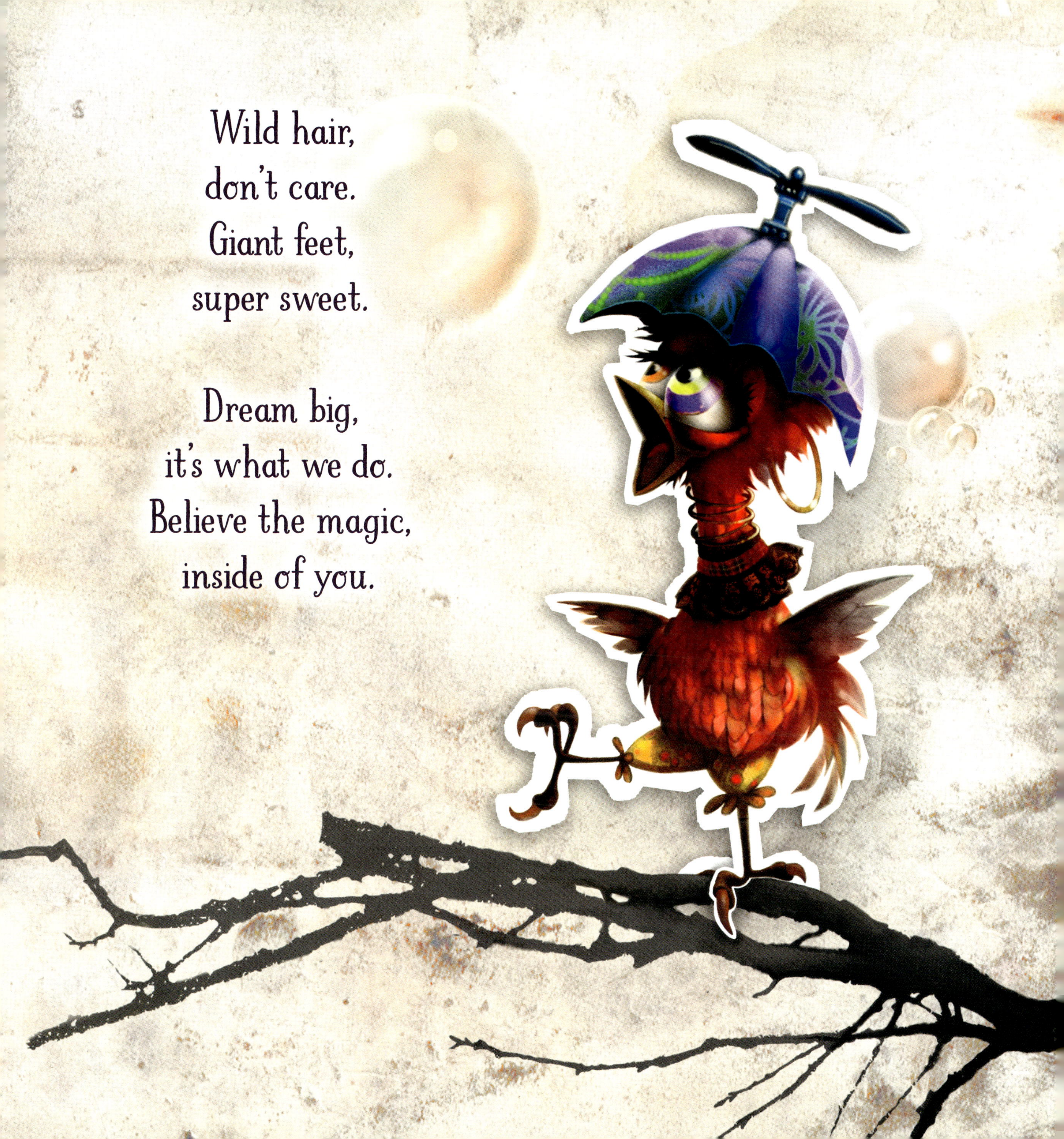

Wild hair,
don't care.
Giant feet,
super sweet.

Dream big,
it's what we do.
Believe the magic,
inside of you.

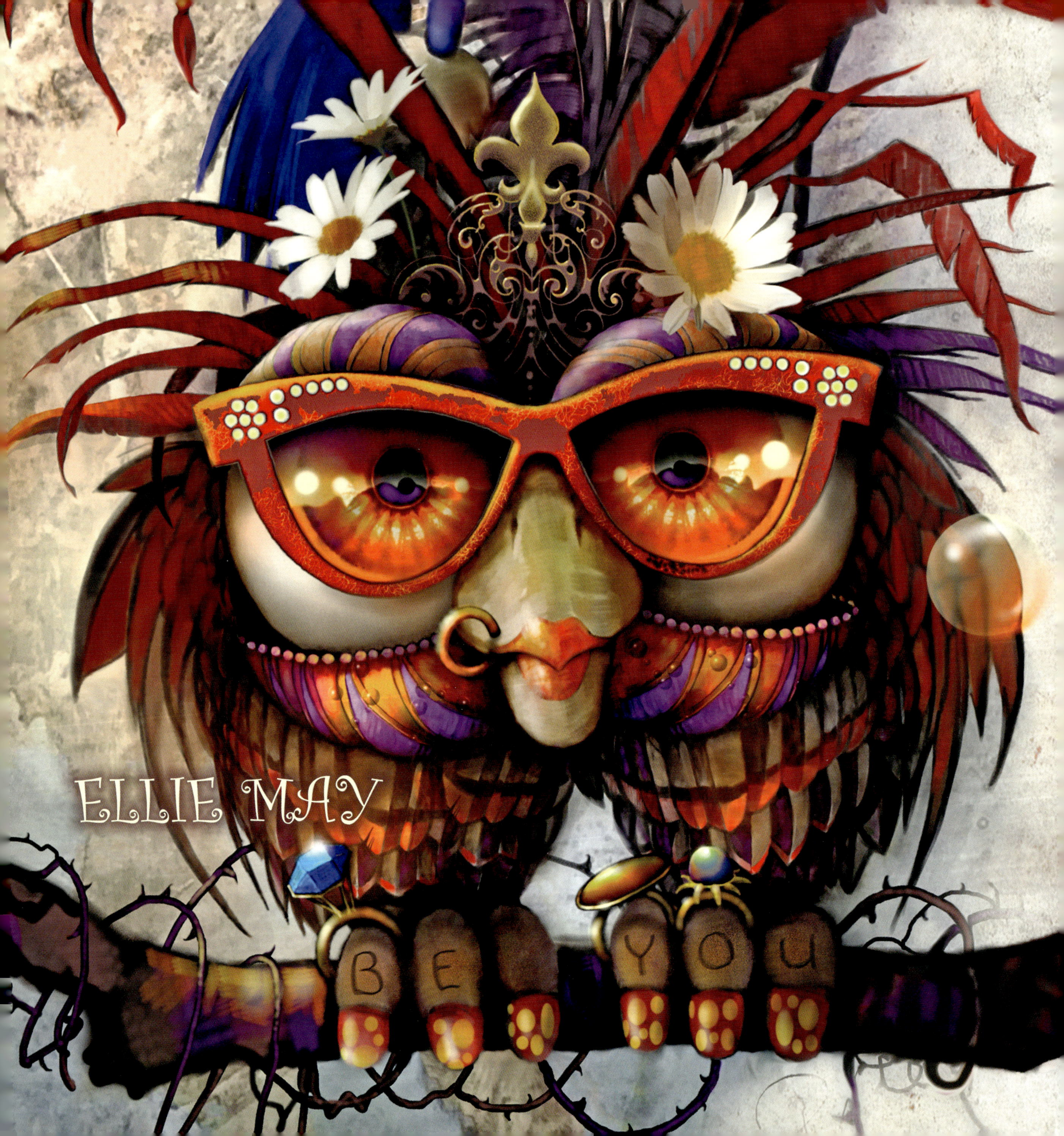
ELLIE MAY
B E
Y O U

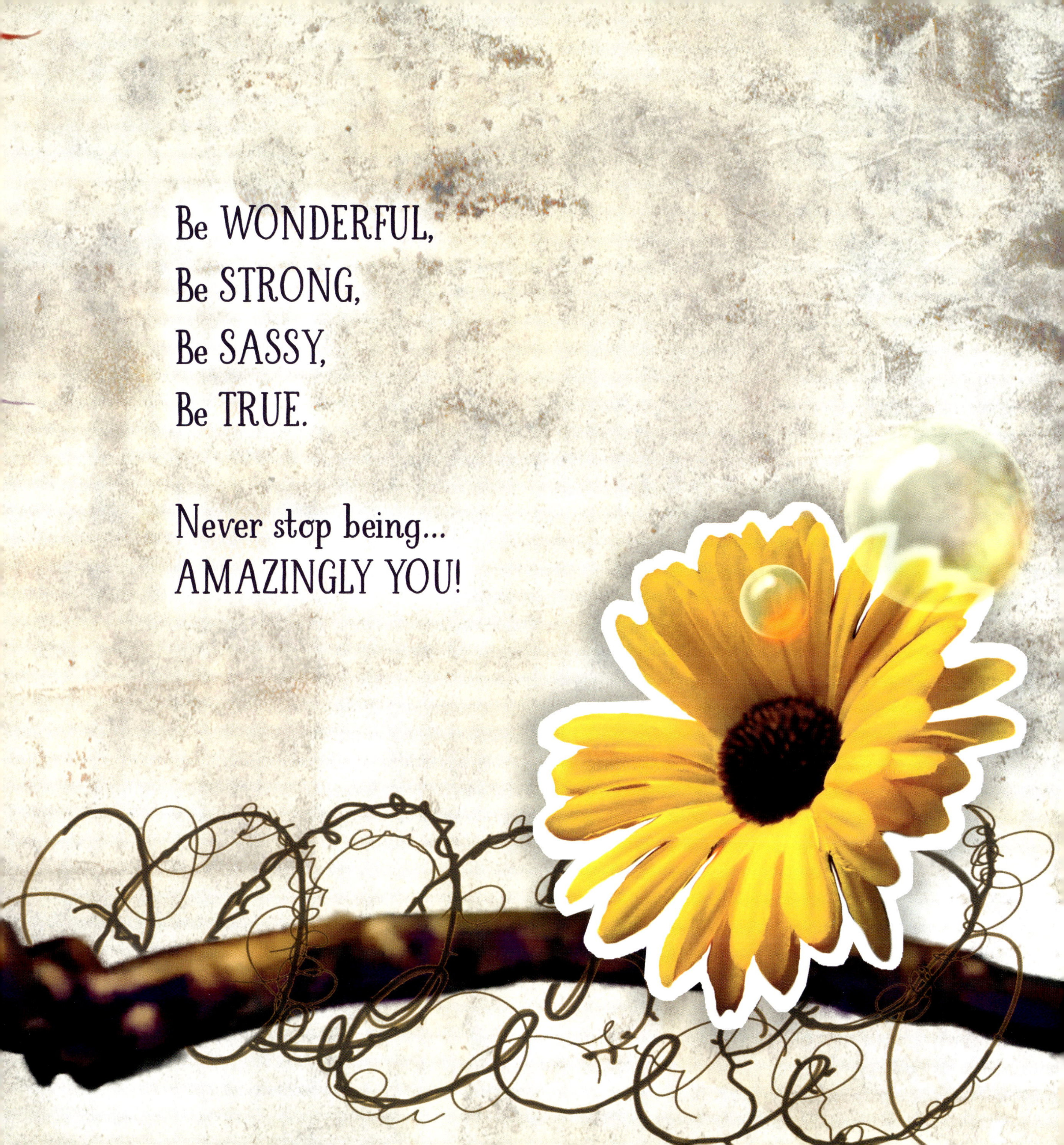

Be WONDERFUL,
Be STRONG,
Be SASSY,
Be TRUE.

Never stop being...
AMAZINGLY YOU!

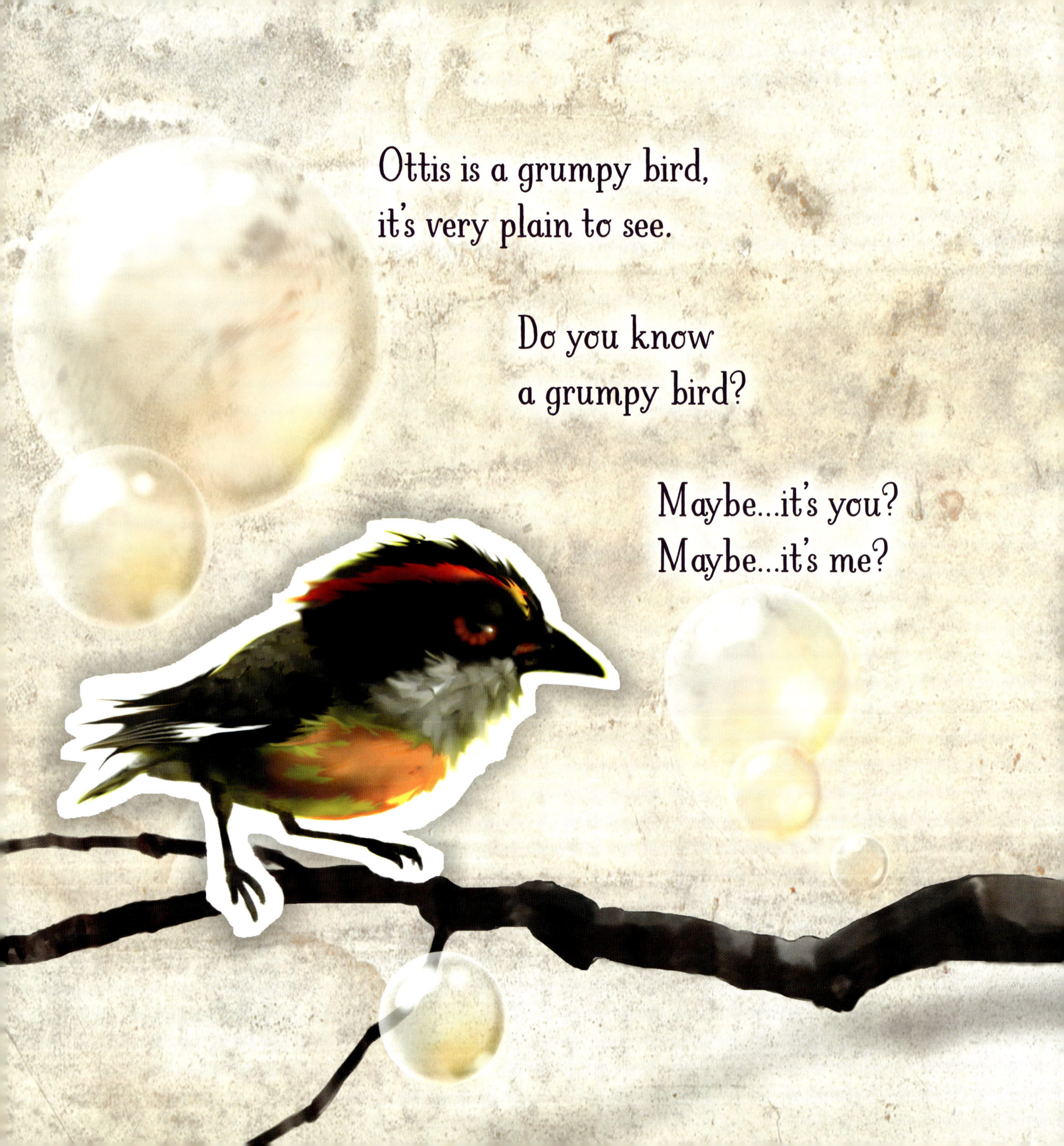

Ottis is a grumpy bird,
it's very plain to see.

Do you know
a grumpy bird?

Maybe...it's you?
Maybe...it's me?

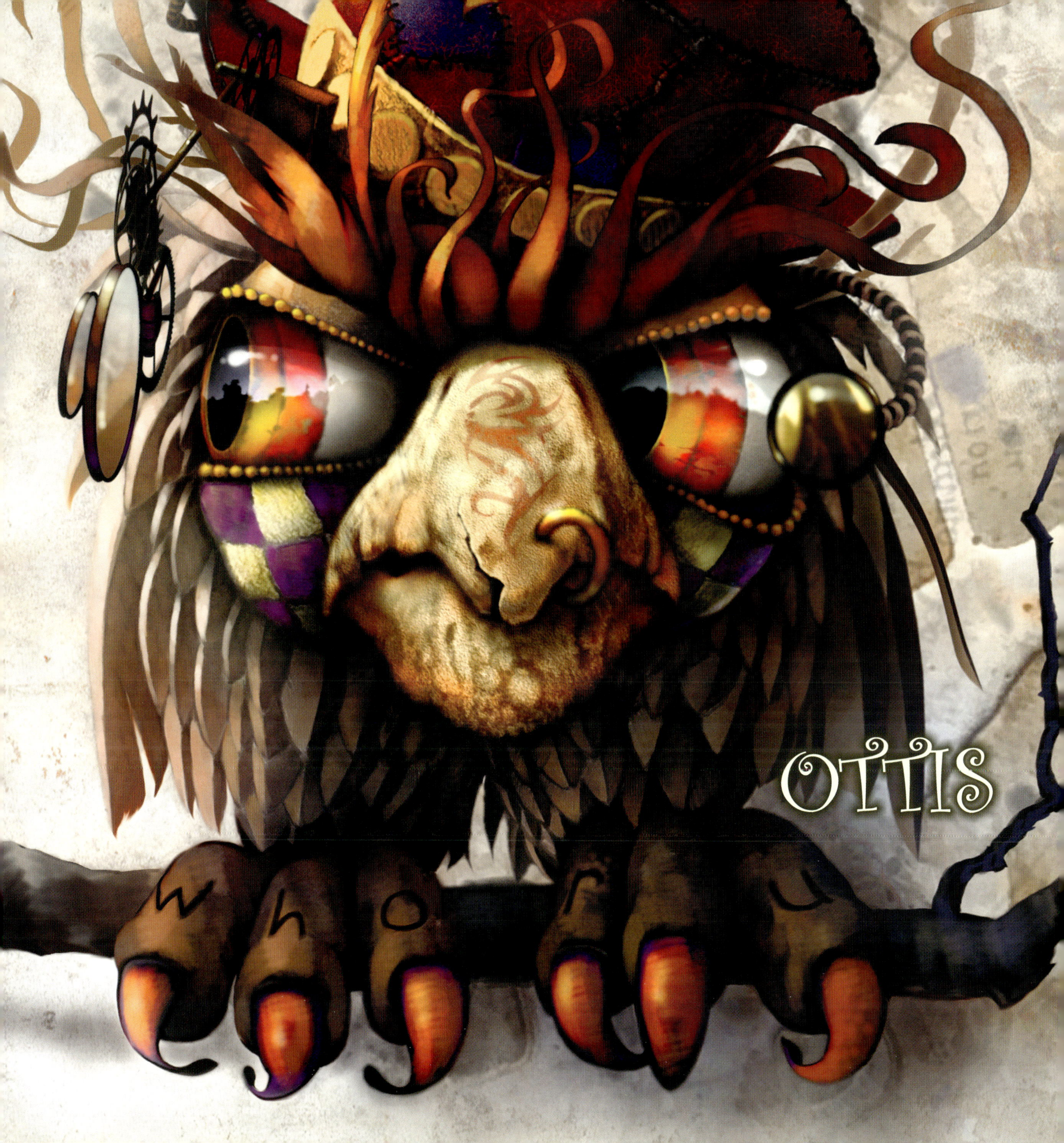
OTTIS

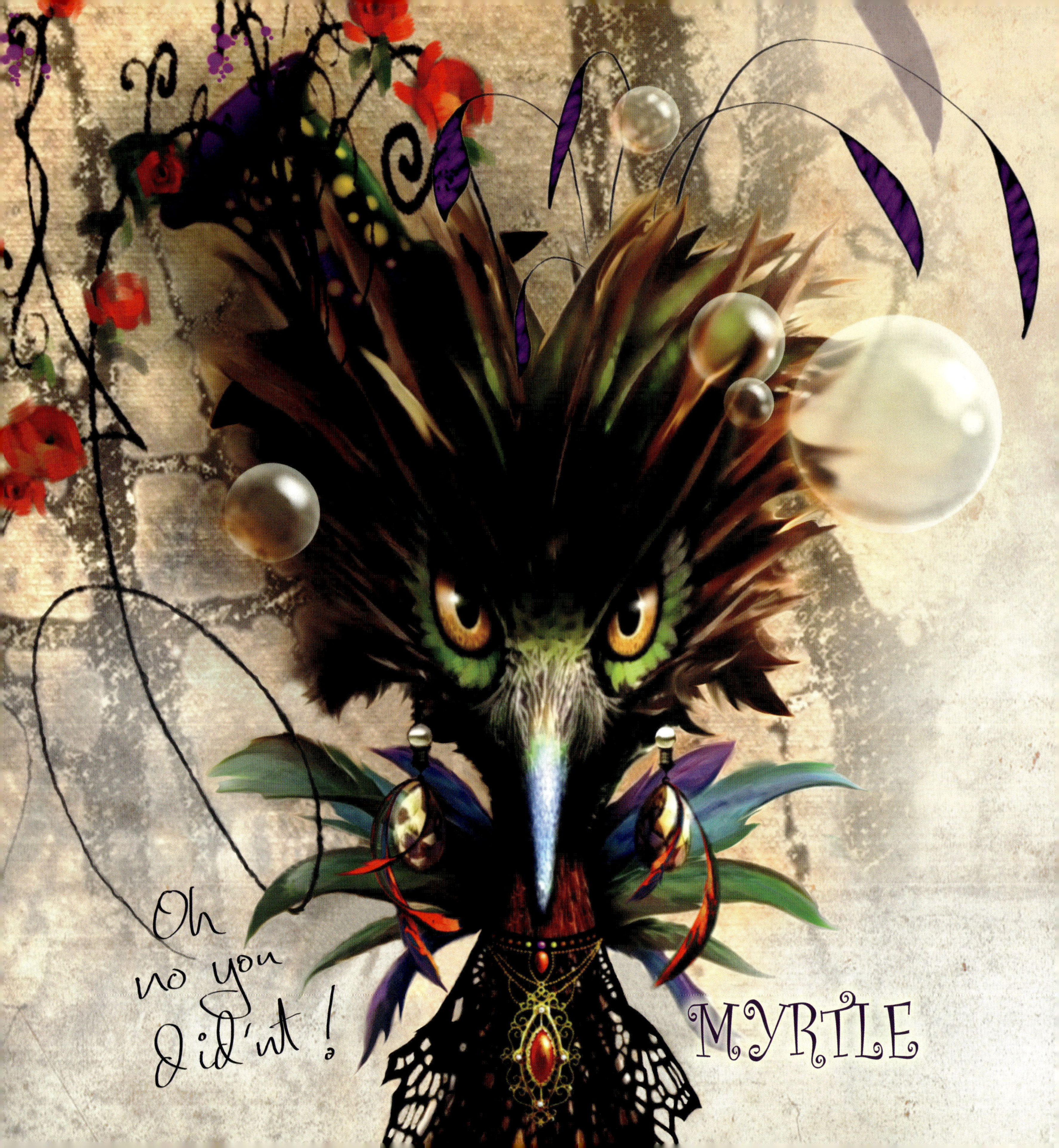
Oh
no you
did'nt!
MYRTLE

Myrtle is
confident and brave.
Her favorite hat
makes her feel this way.

She never worries,
what others say.
She wears her hat
anyway.

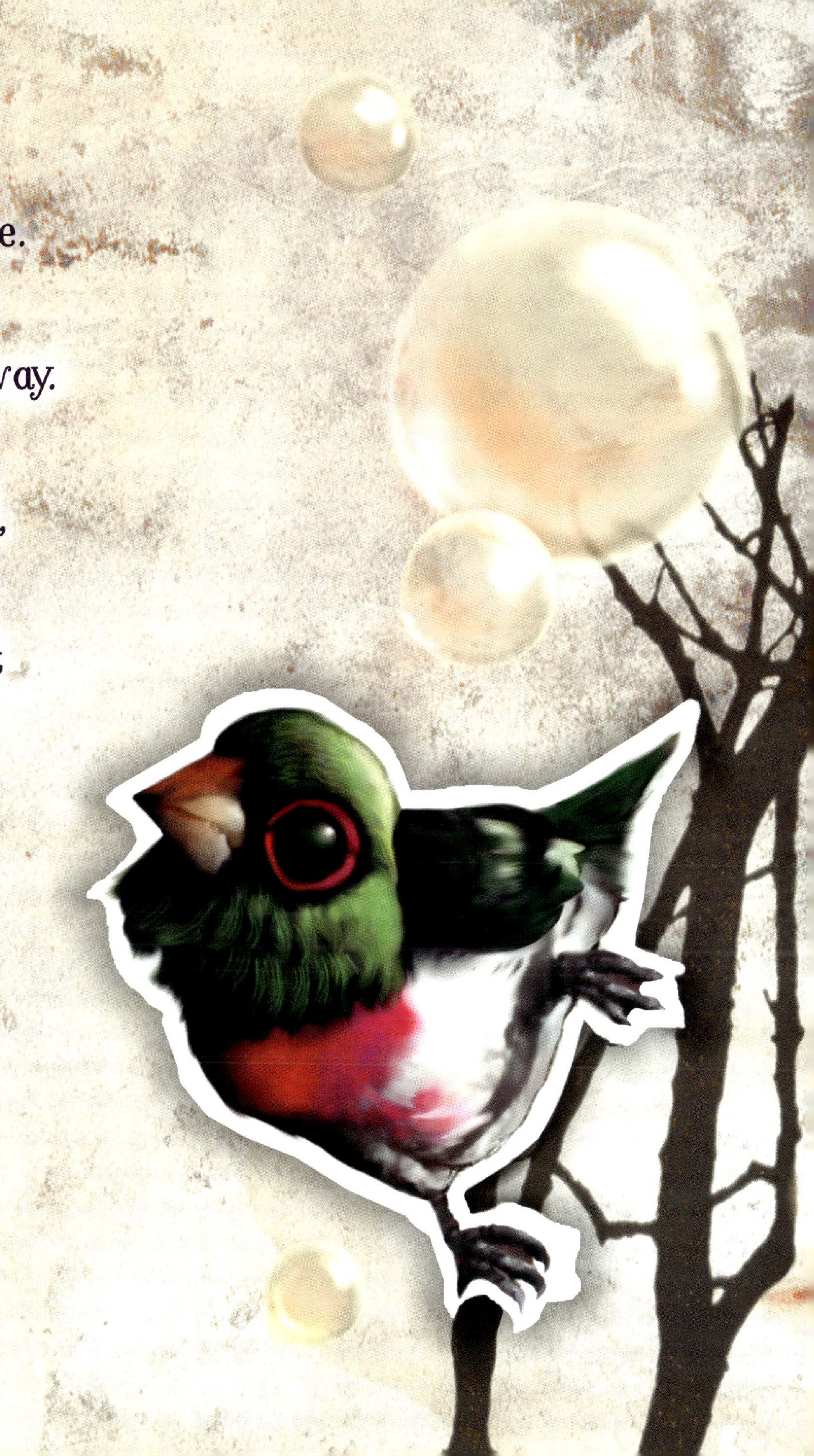

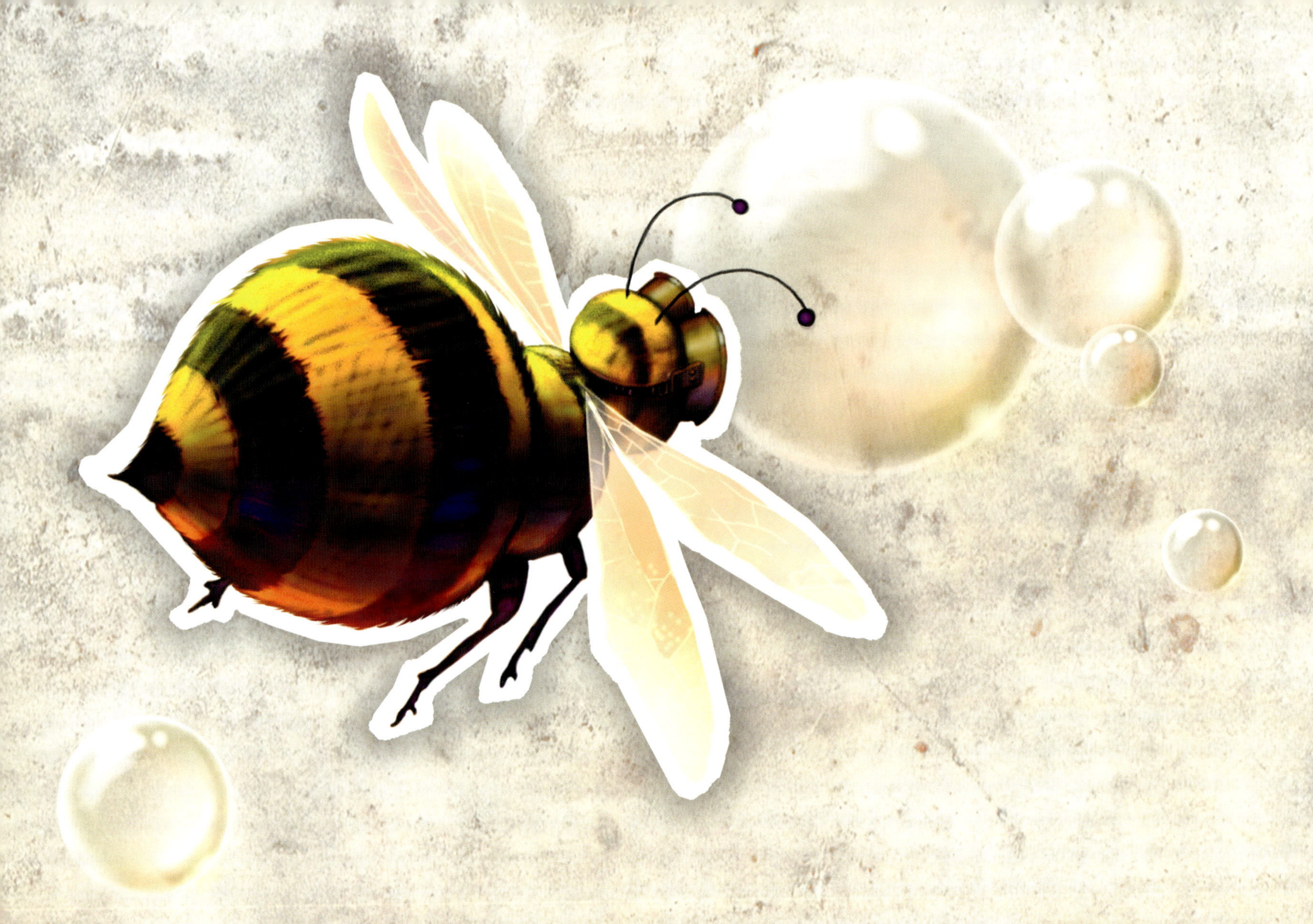

No excuses...
you will hear.
Her opinions...
are quite clear.

A little sassy
this is true.
Just a bird
with attitude.

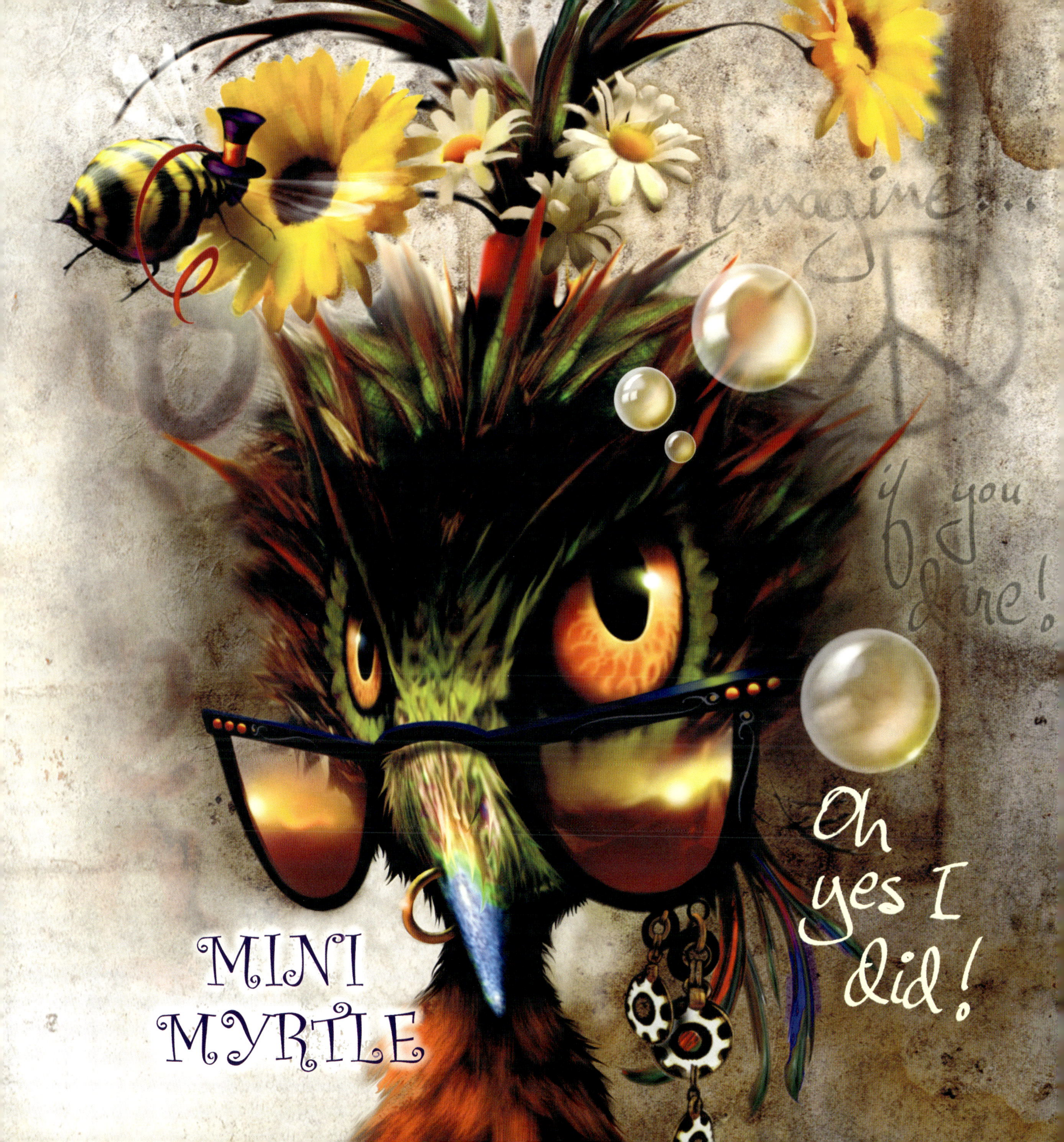
imagine...
if you dare!
Oh yes I did!
MINI MYRTLE

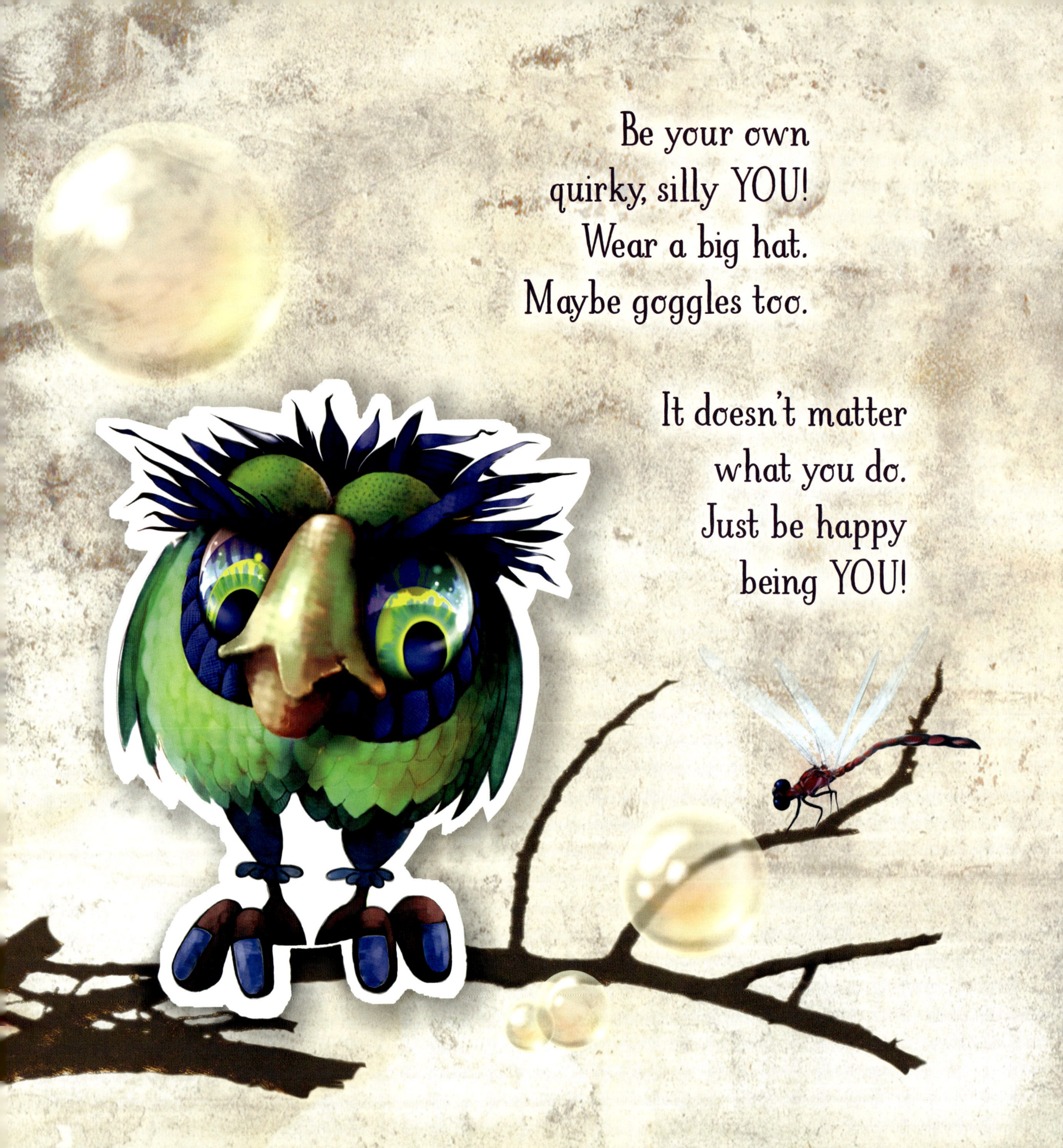

Be your own
quirky, silly YOU!
Wear a big hat.
Maybe goggles too.

It doesn't matter
what you do.
Just be happy
being YOU!

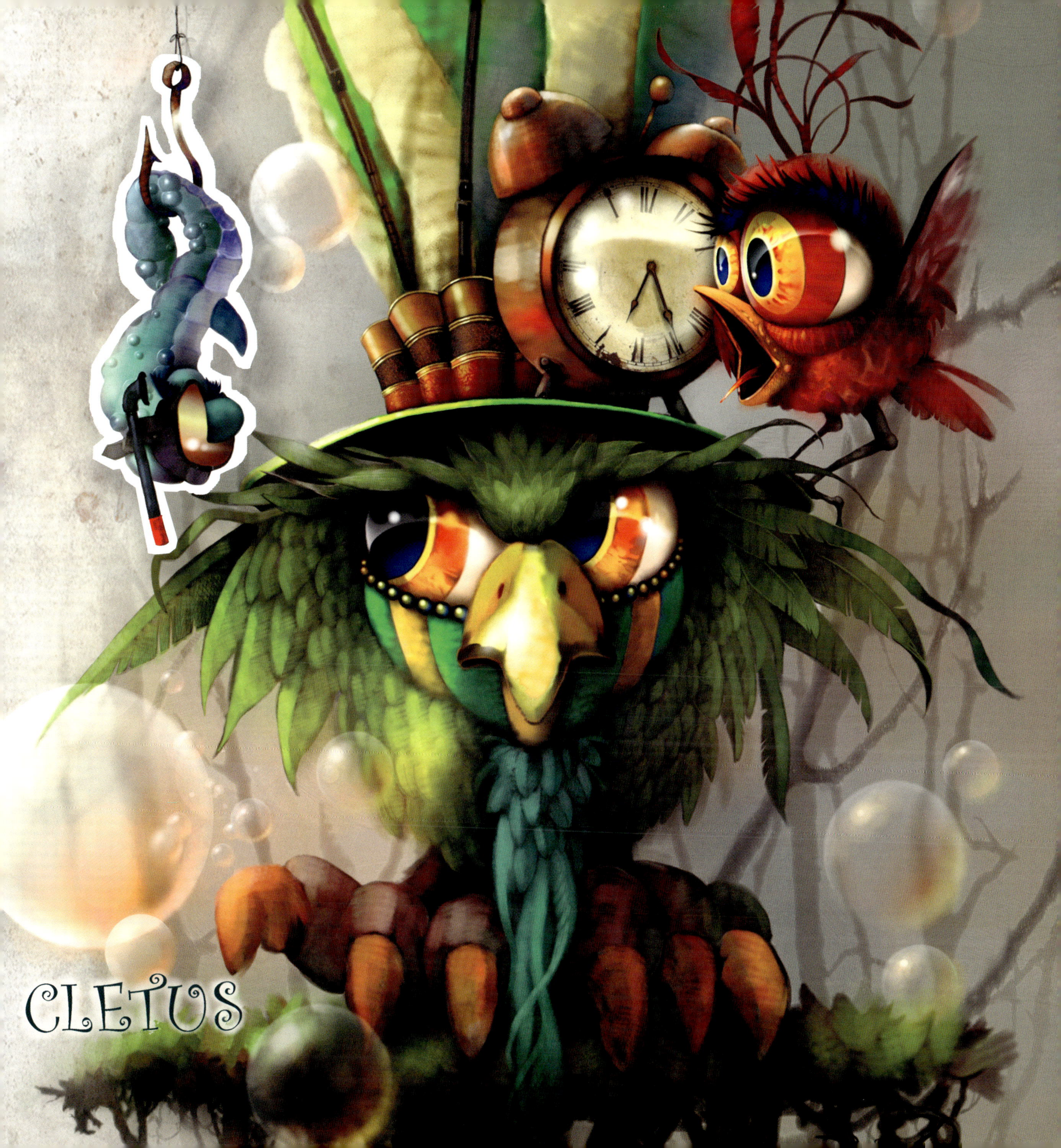
CLETUS

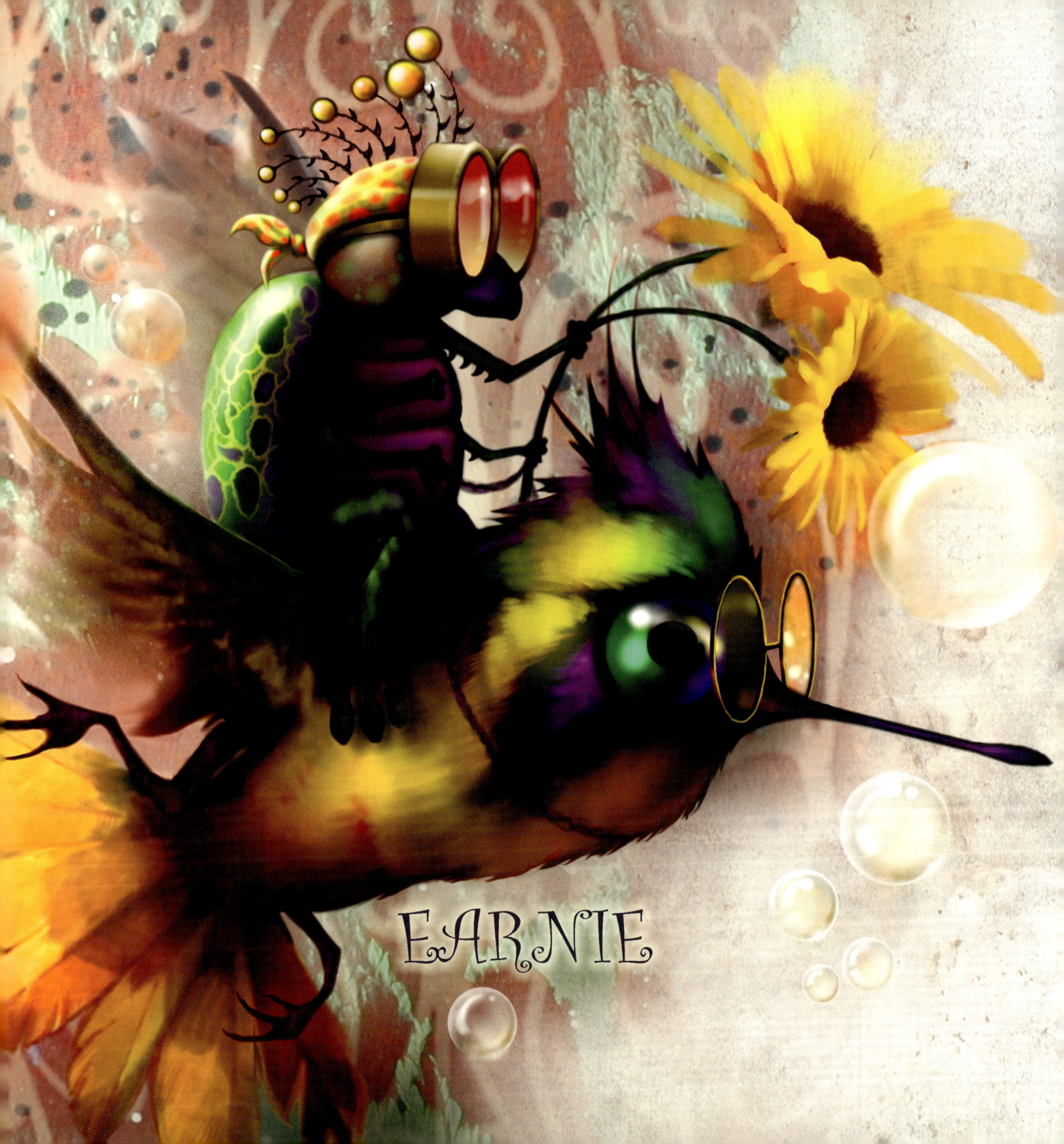
EARNIE

Let's discover something wonderful and new...

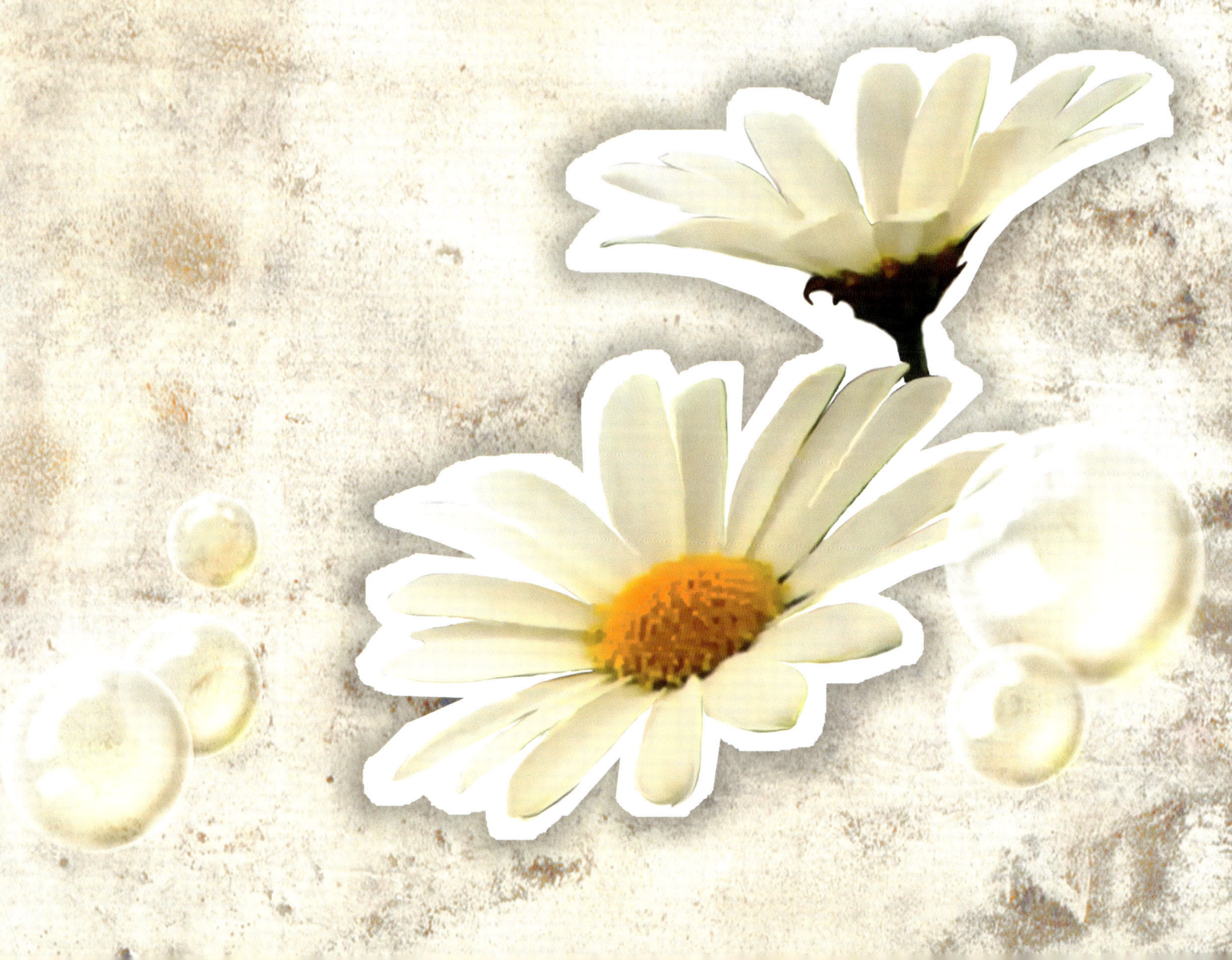

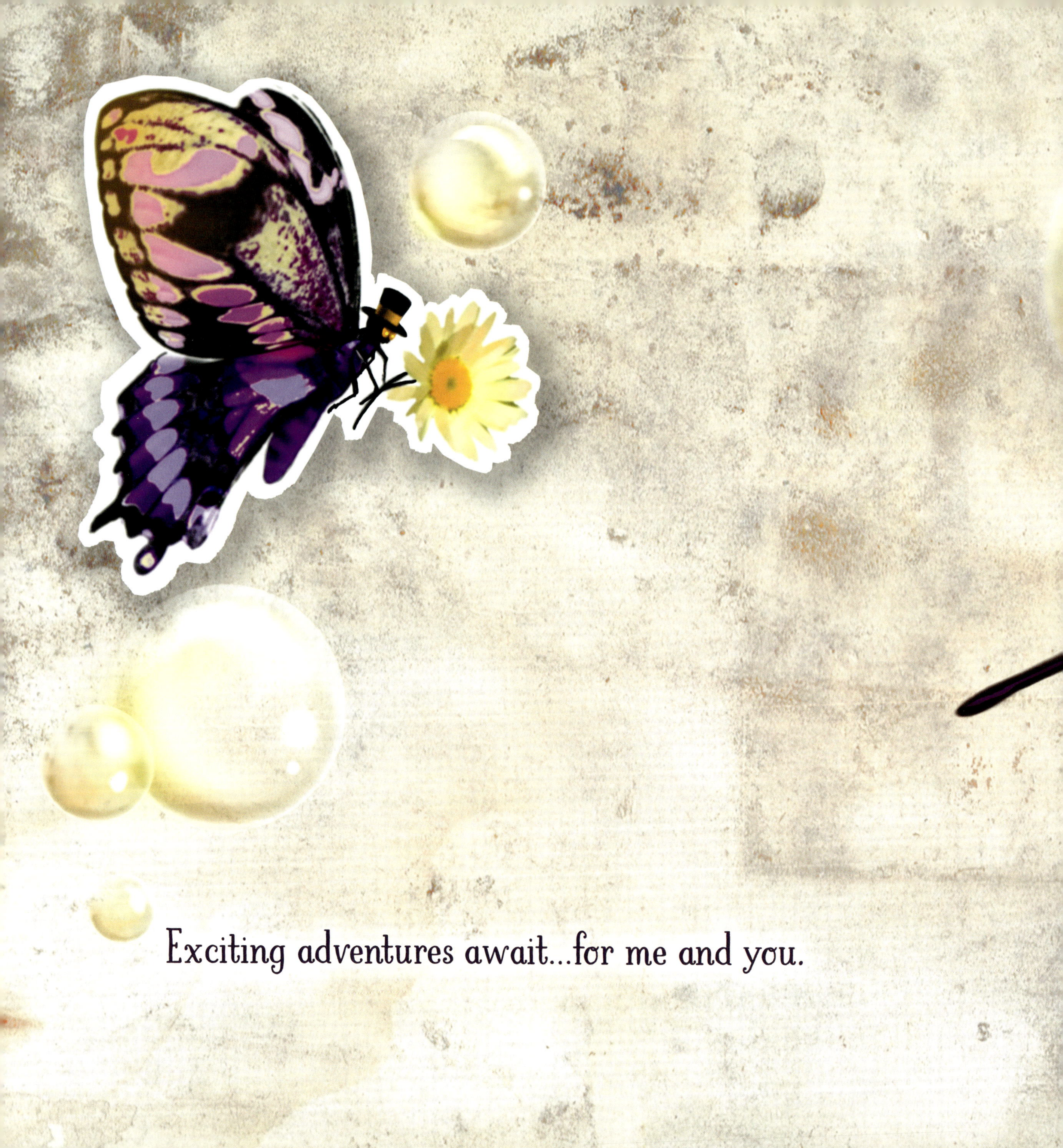

Exciting adventures await...for me and you.

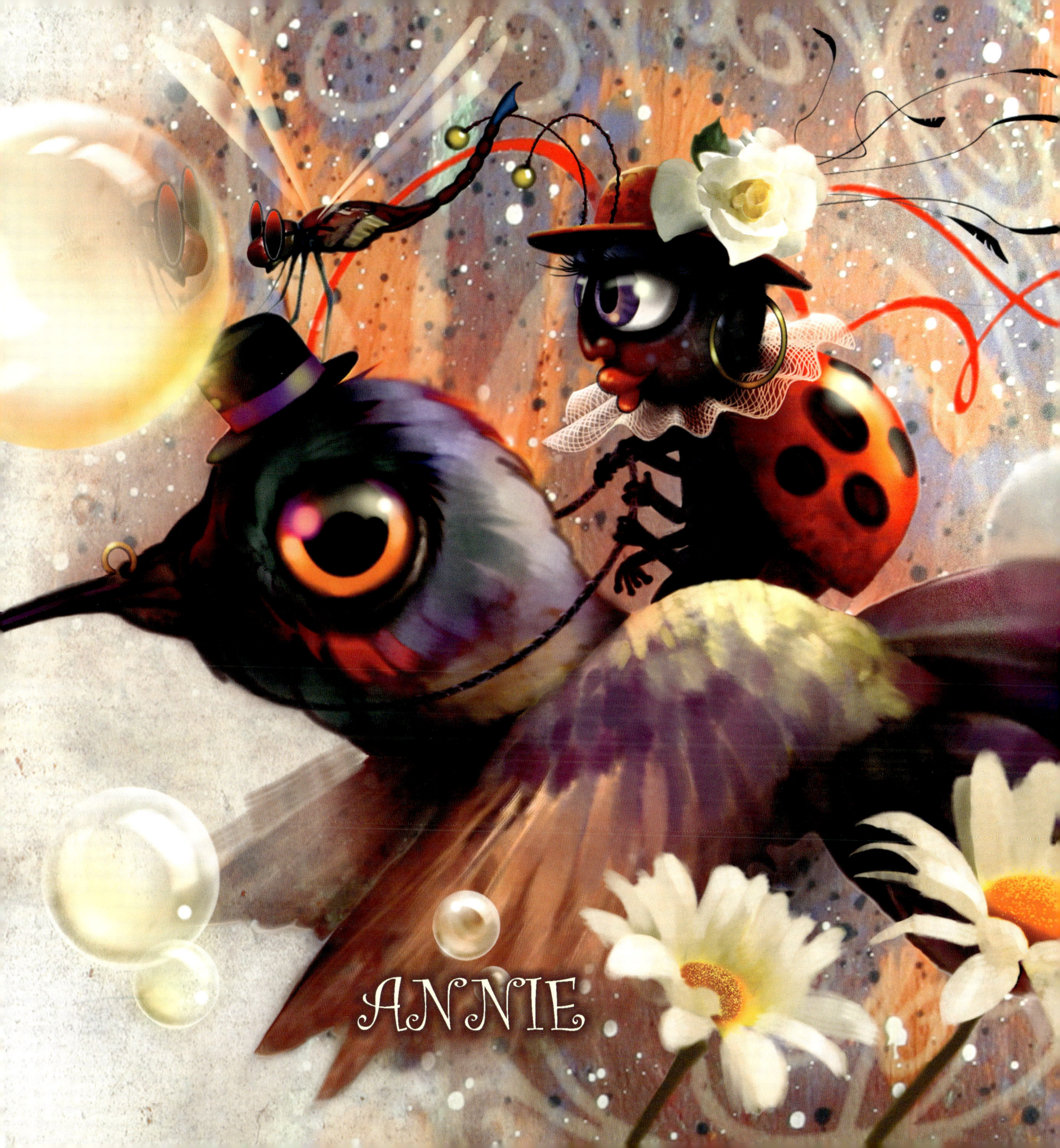
ANNIE

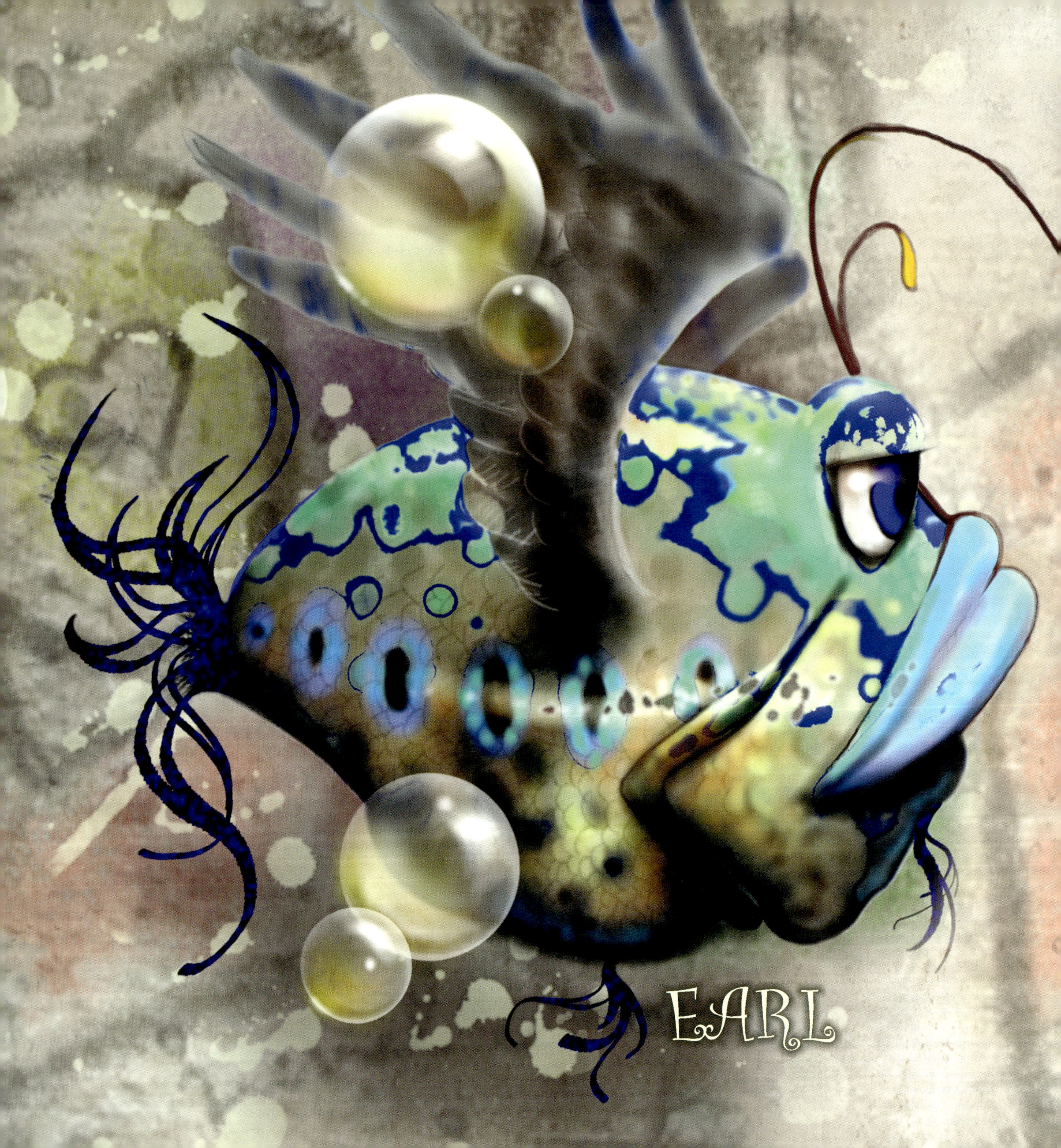
EARL

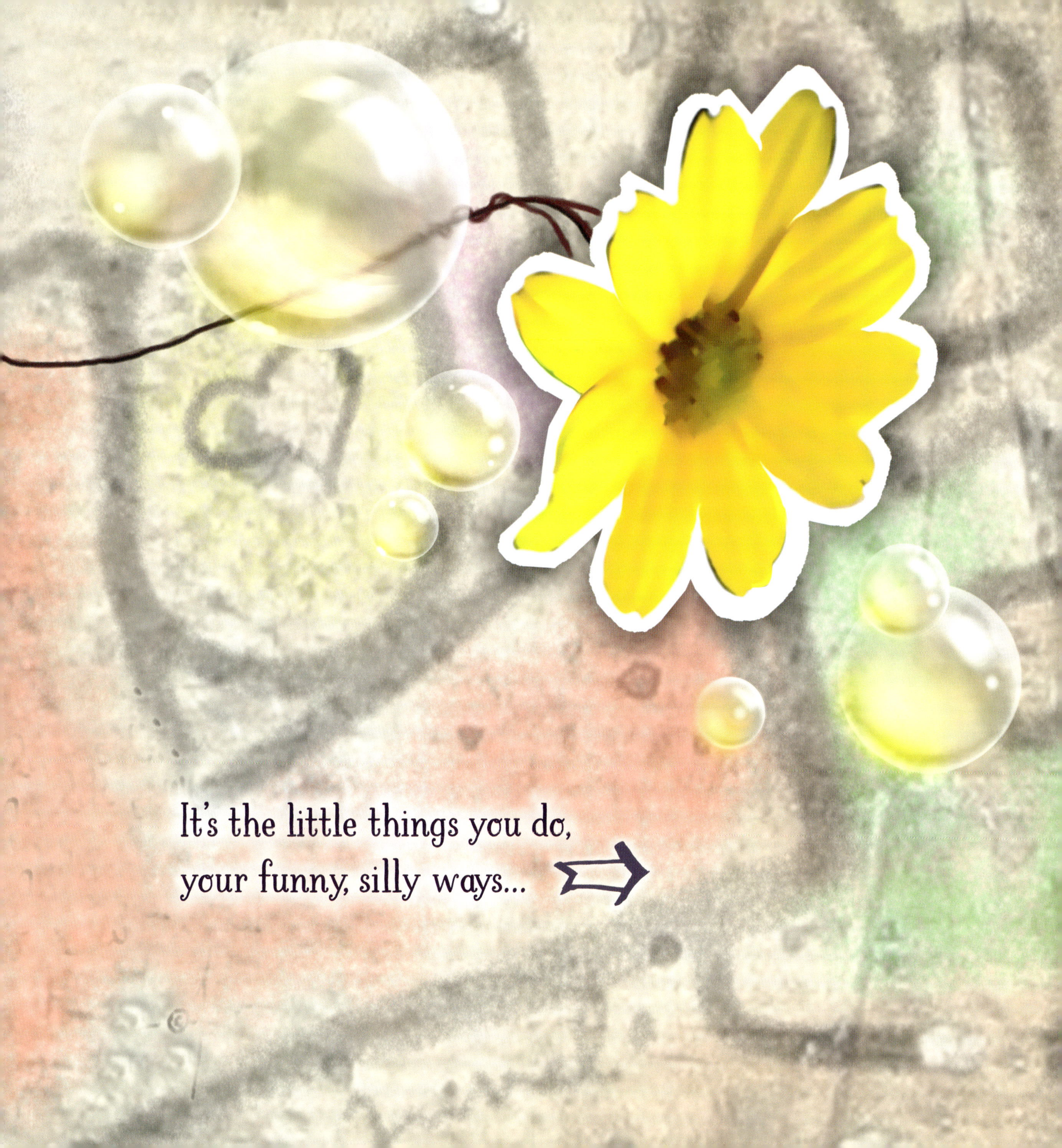

It's the little things you do,
your funny, silly ways...

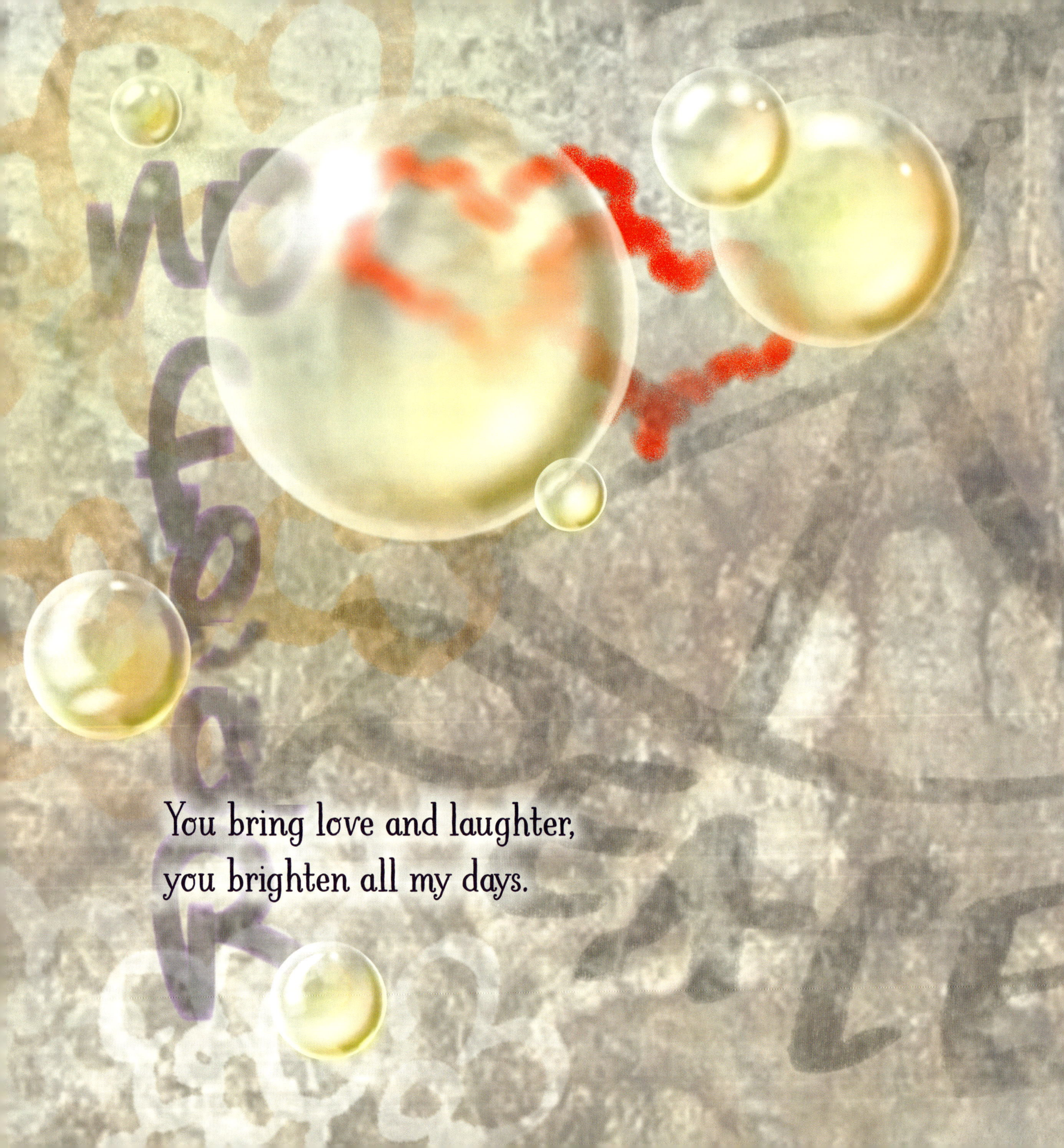

You bring love and laughter,
you brighten all my days.

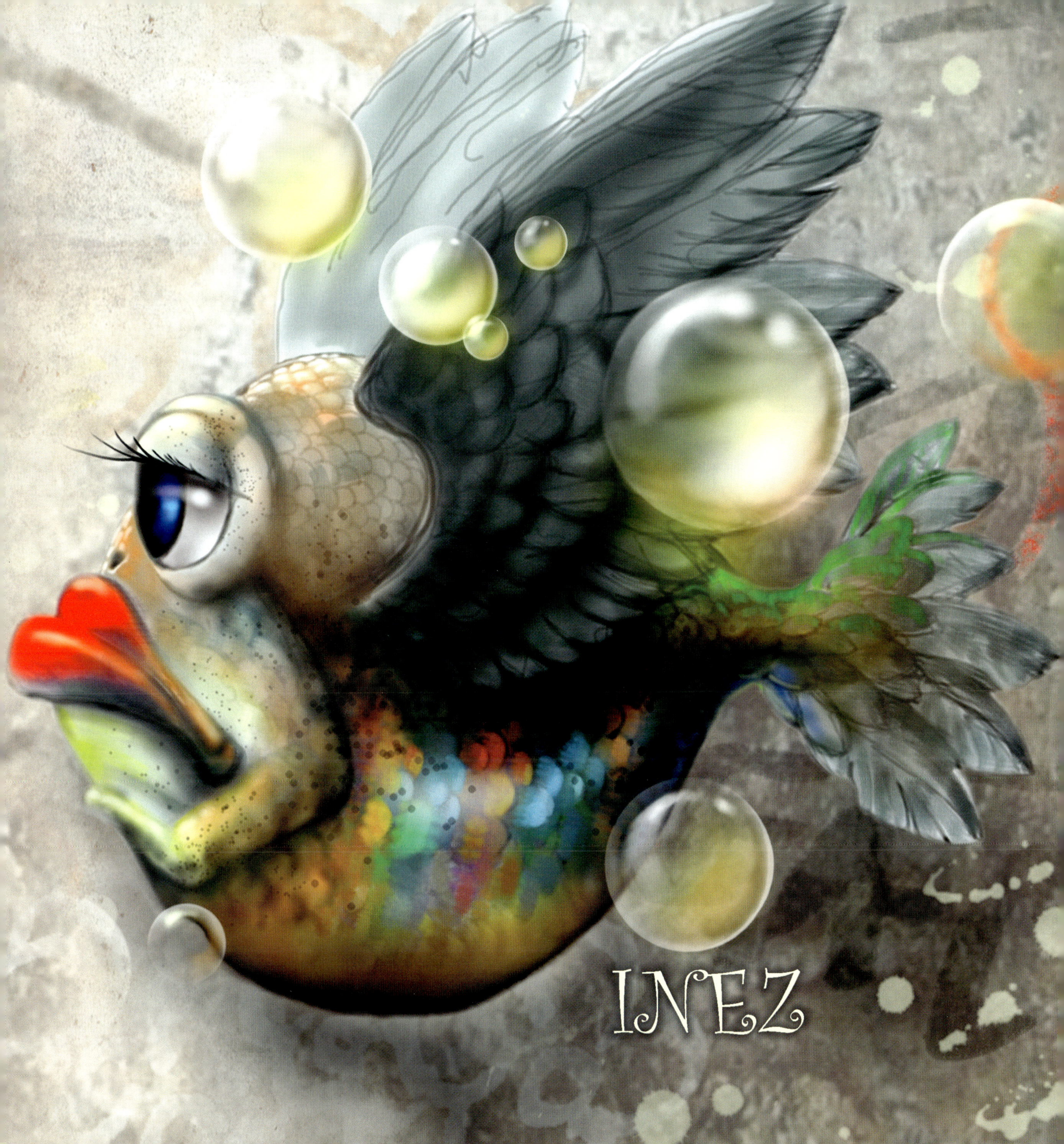
INEZ

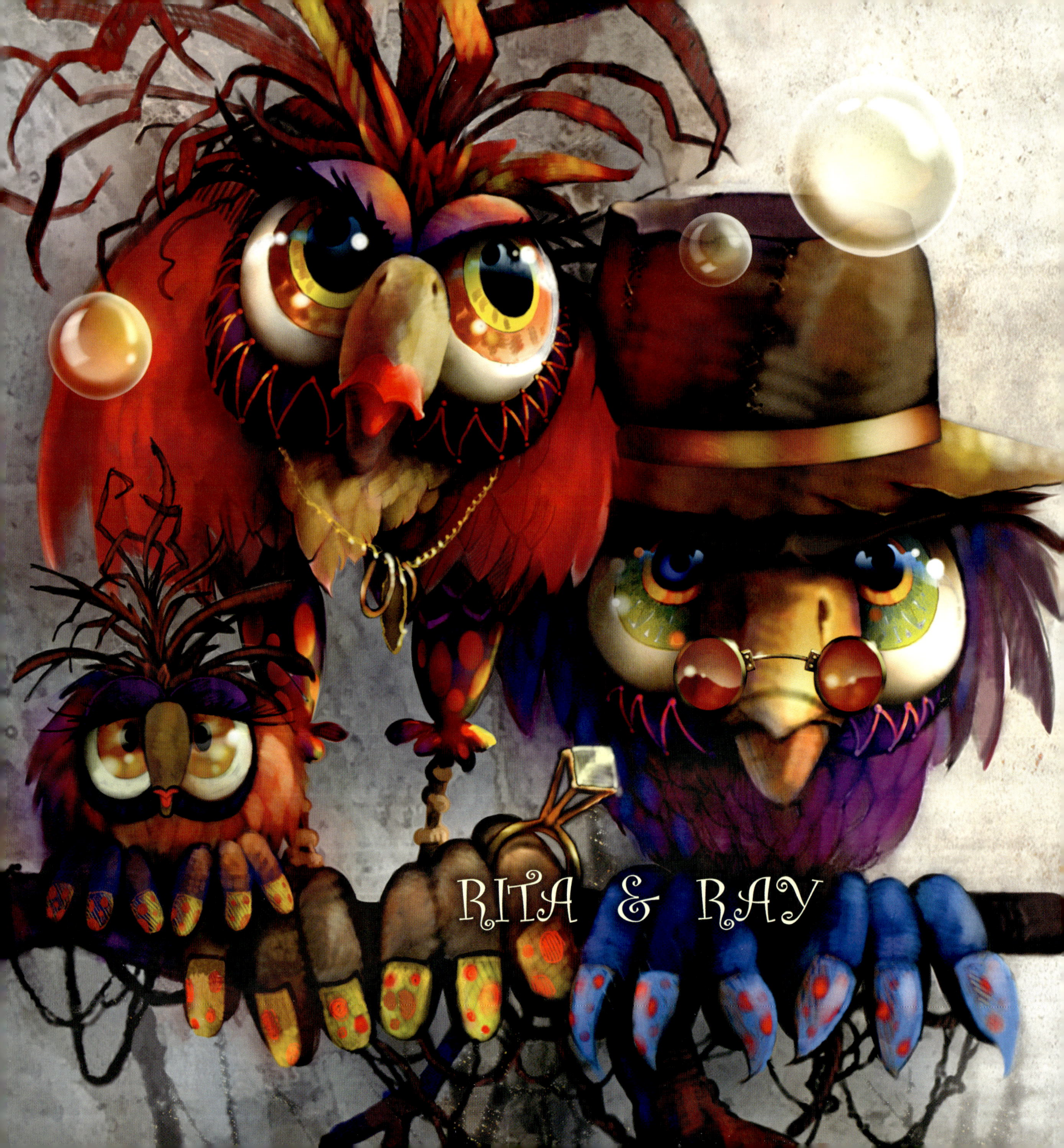
RITA & RAY

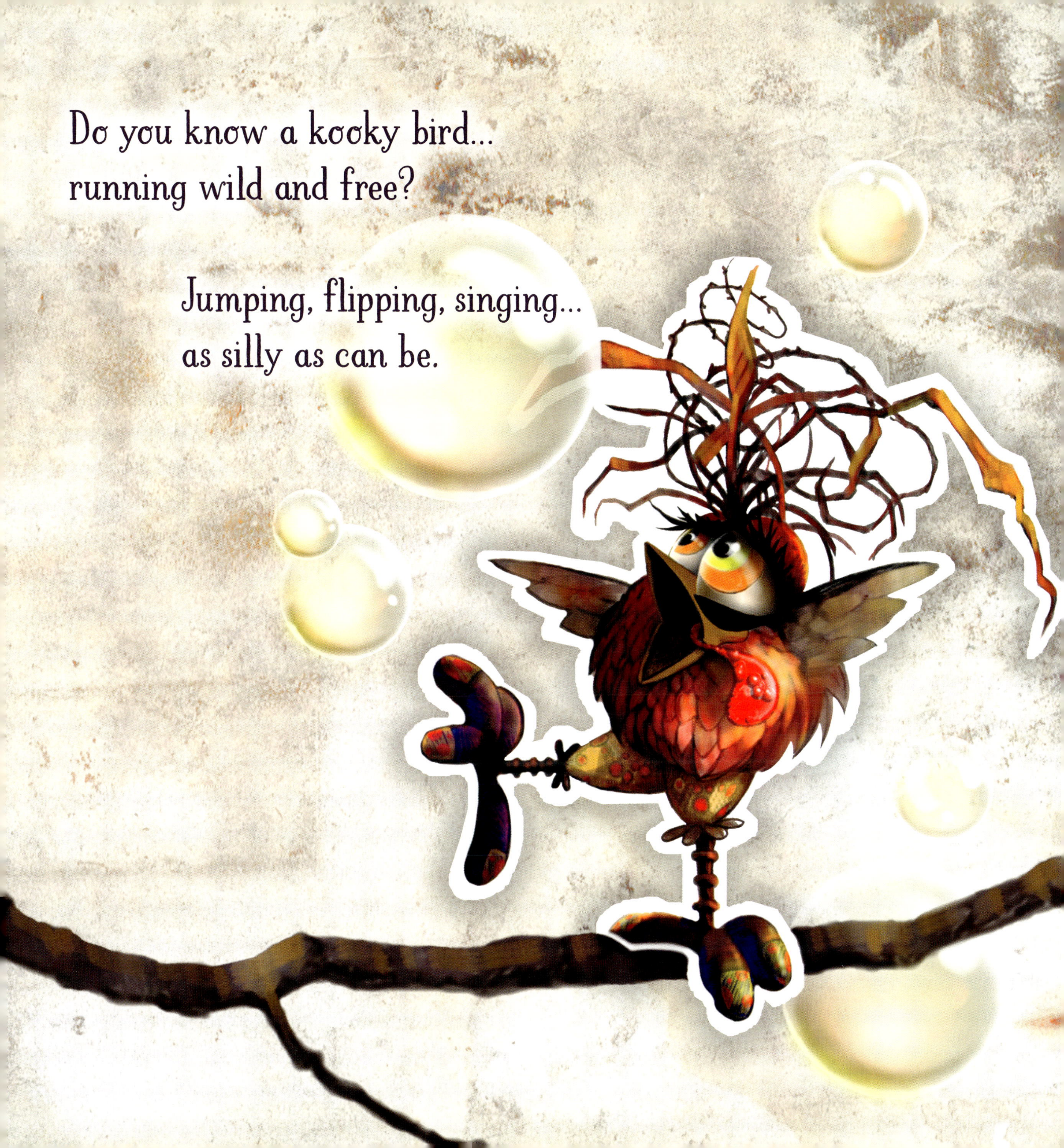

Do you know a kooky bird...
running wild and free?

Jumping, flipping, singing...
as silly as can be.

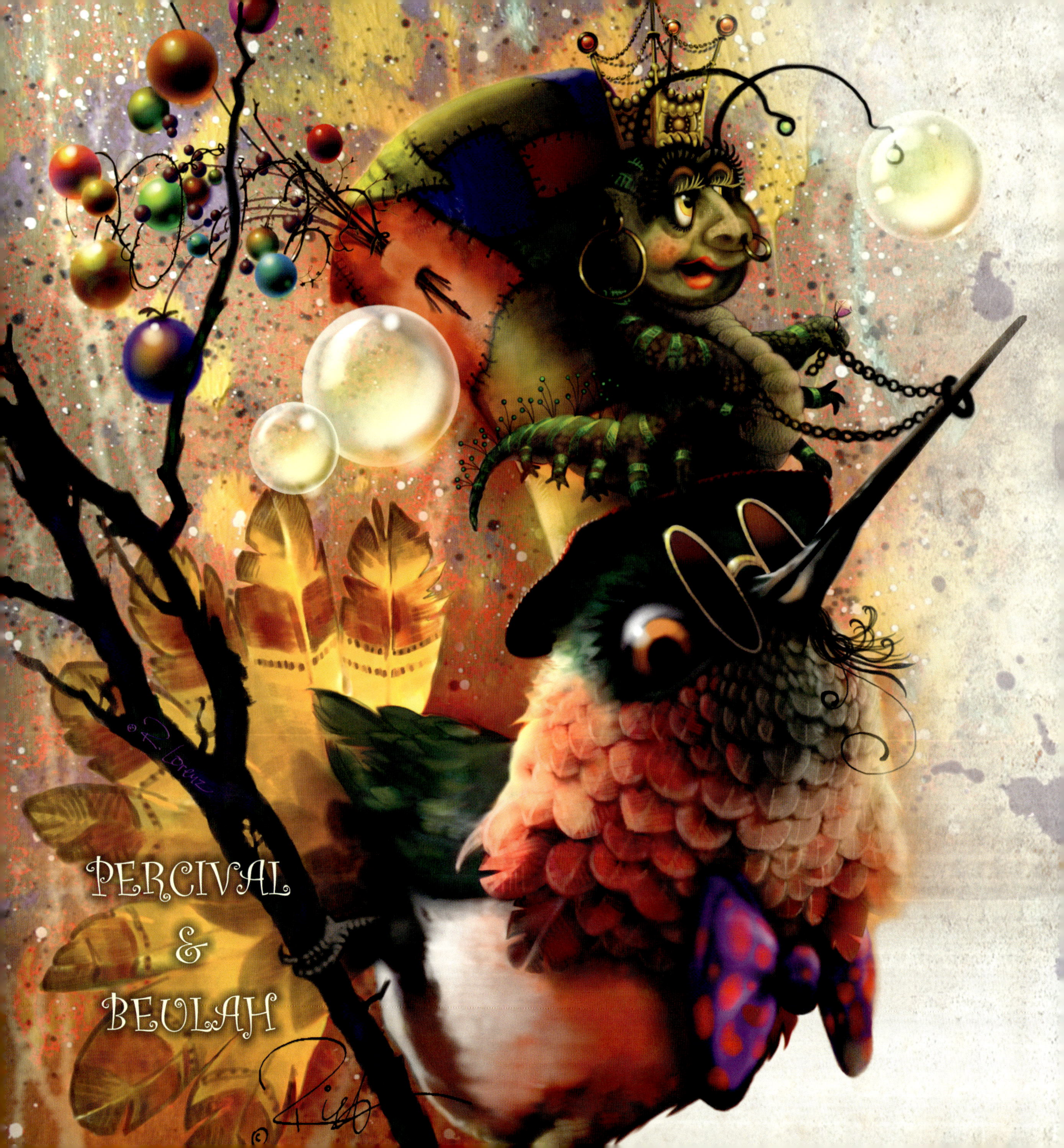
PERCIVAL
&
BEULAH

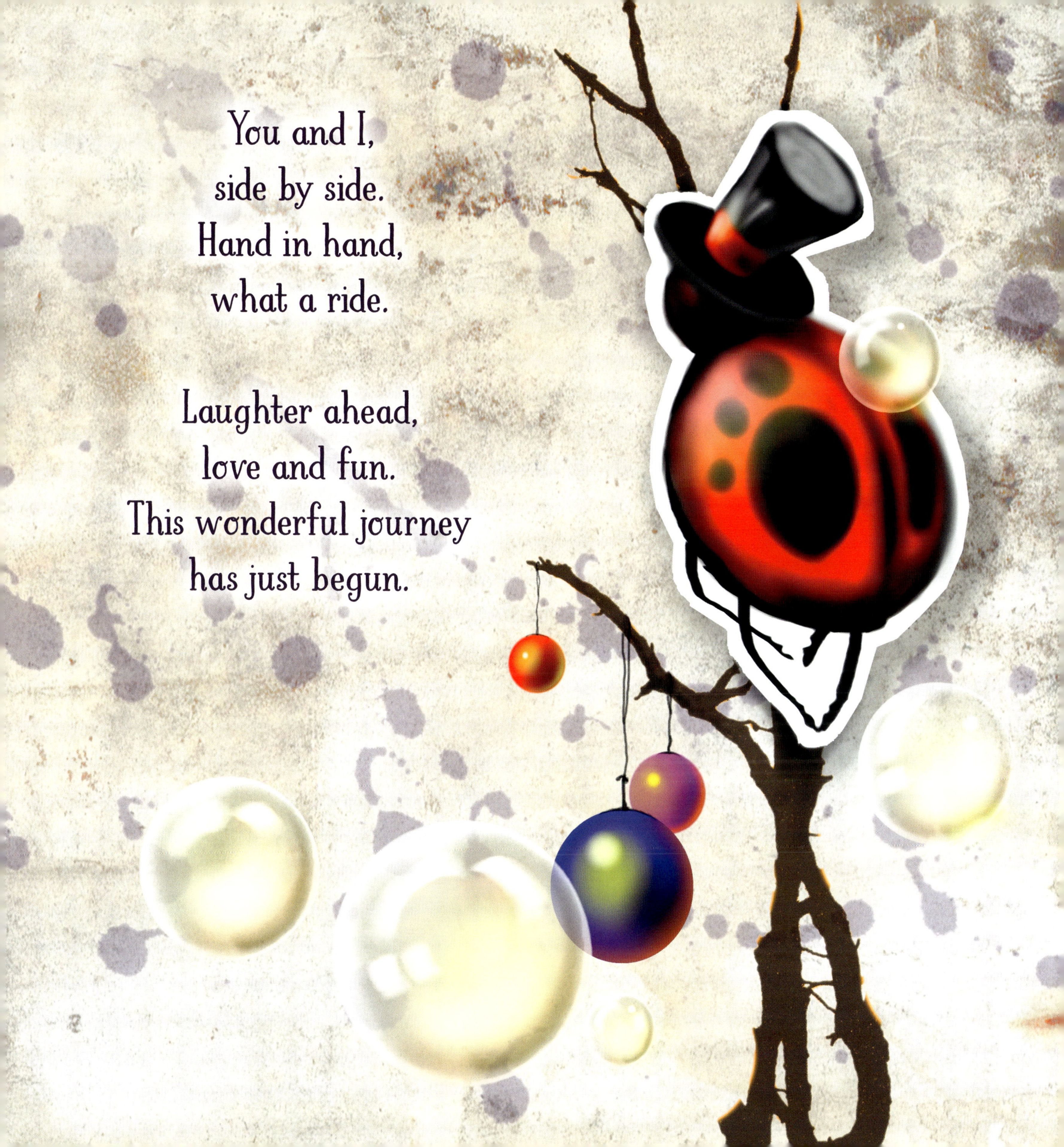

You and I,
side by side.
Hand in hand,
what a ride.

Laughter ahead,
love and fun.
This wonderful journey
has just begun.

# WHICH BIRD...

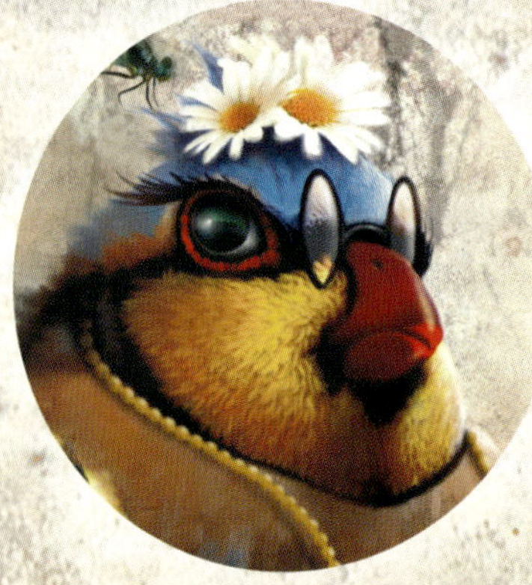

Fearless

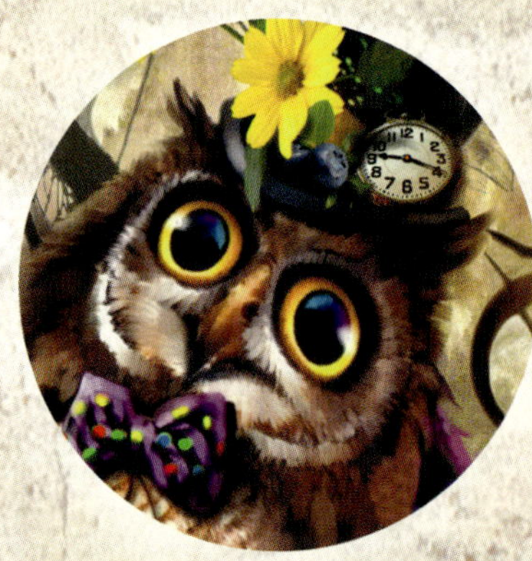

Adorable

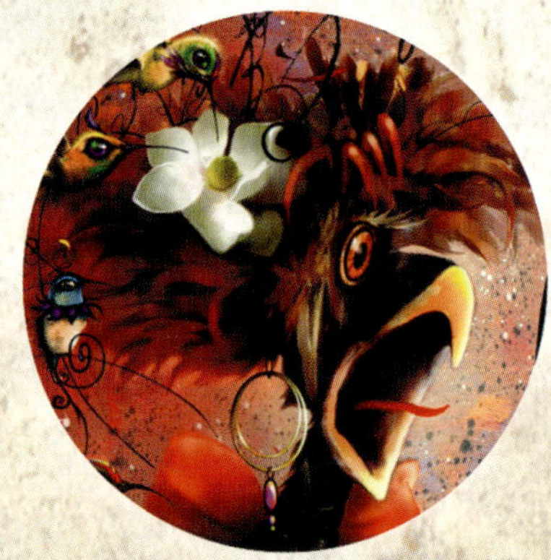

Dramatic

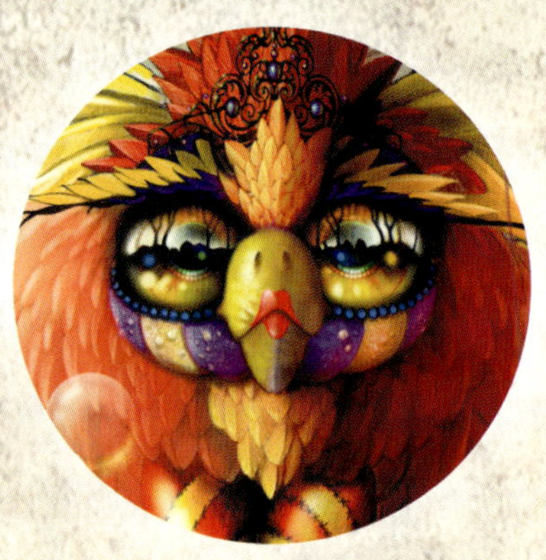

Confident

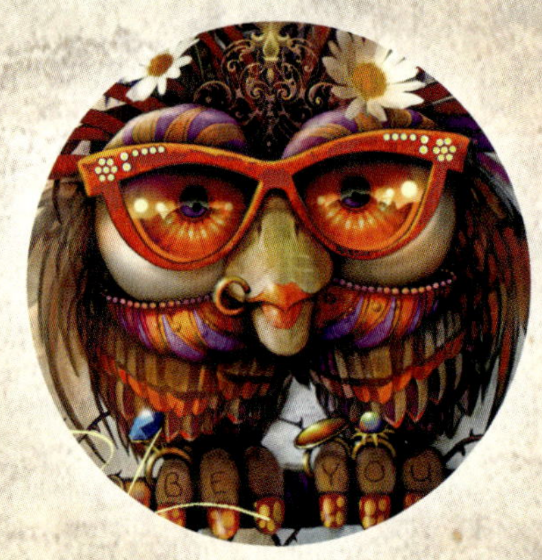

Sassy

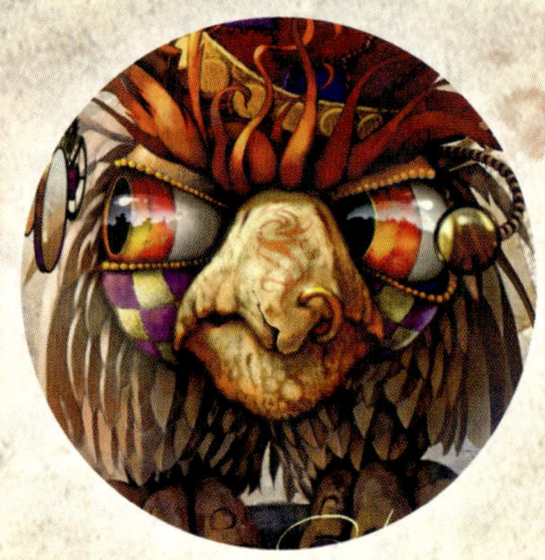

Grumpy

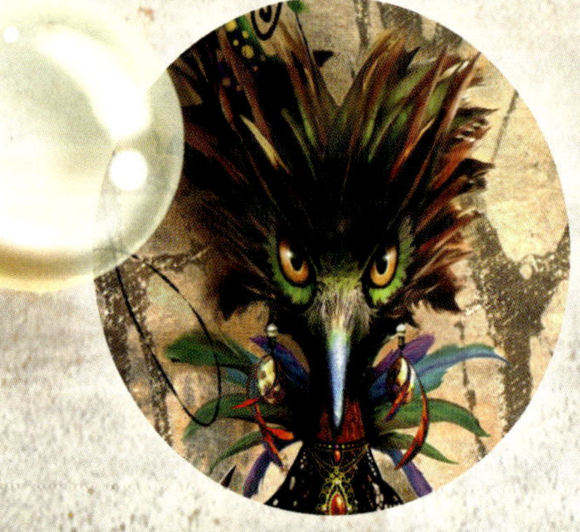

Intense

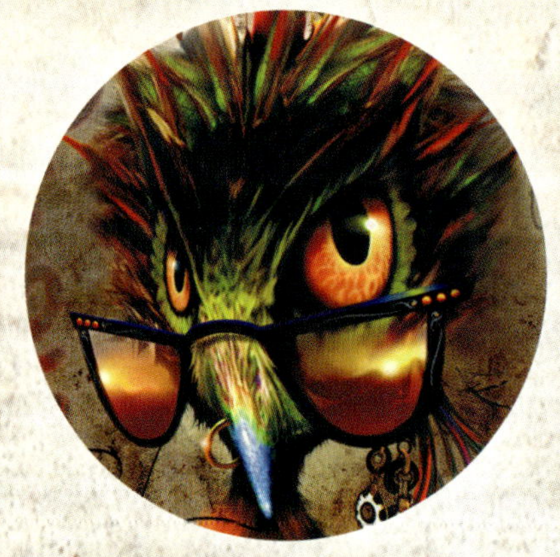

Daring

# ARE YOU?

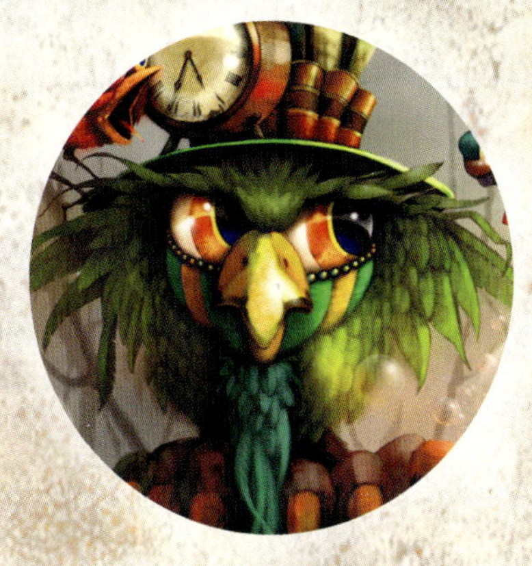

Adventurous

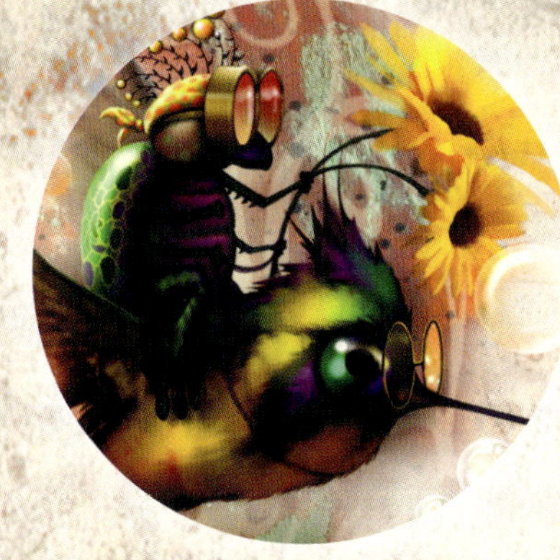

Friendly

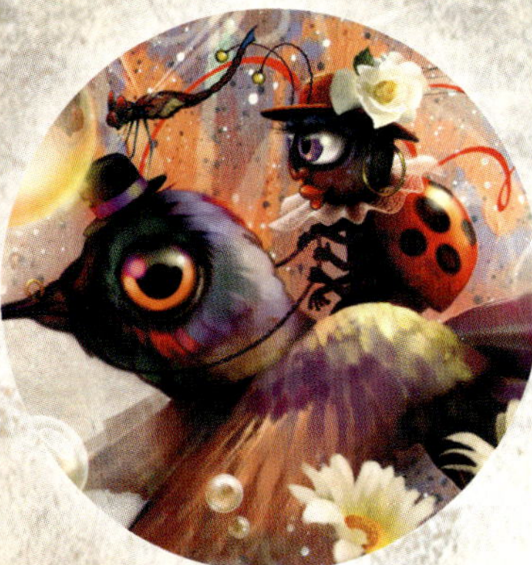

Happy

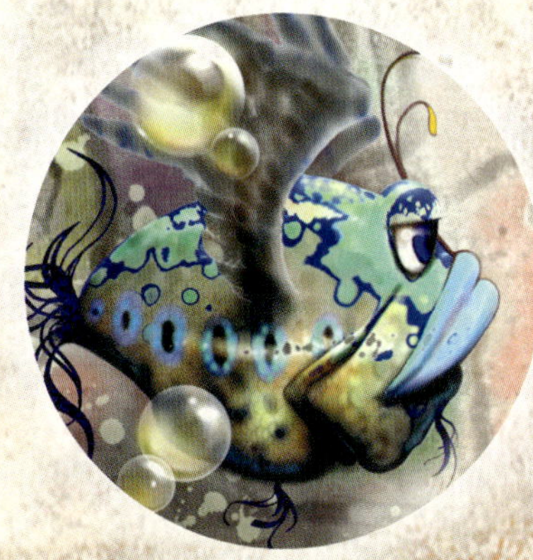

Dreamer

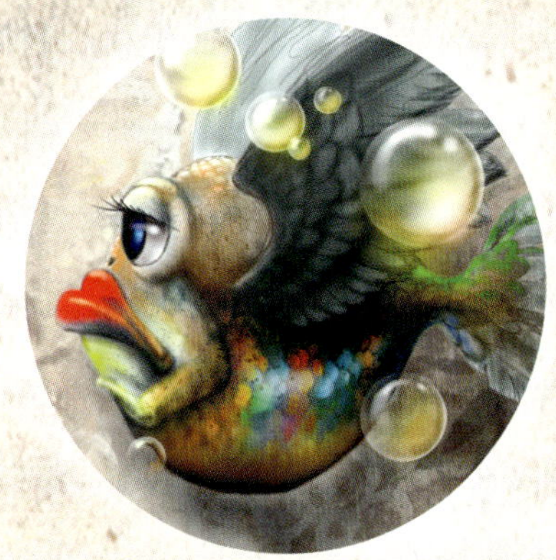

Creative

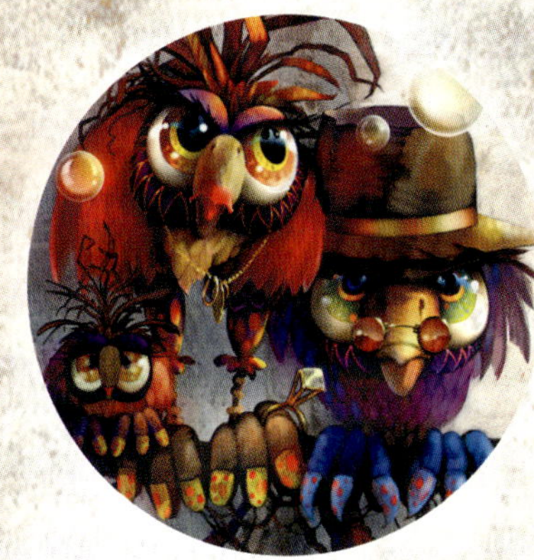

Loved

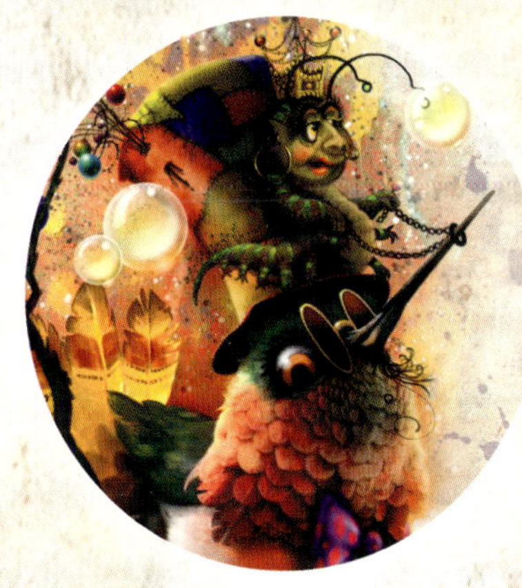

Caring

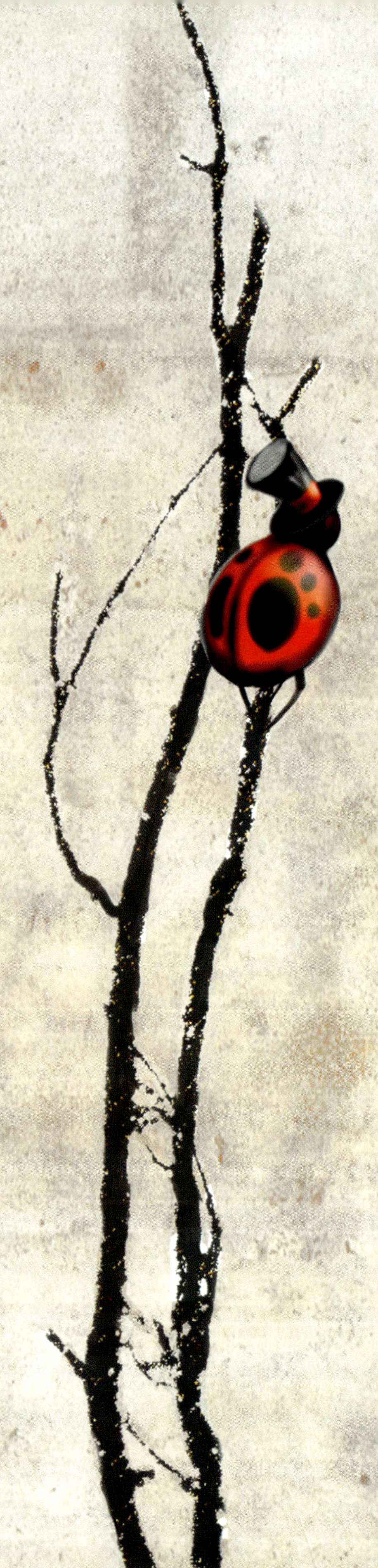

# Welcome to Our World

It's not every day
we see birds fly by.

We forget to look up
as they soar the open sky.

Each bird has a lesson.
Listen close and you will hear.

Their wisdom and knowledge,
becomes quite clear.

Some birds are funny,
making us giggle and laugh.

Others are grumpy,
though that will never last.

Our feathered friends
are teachers in every way.

Encouraging us to learn,
spread our wings, and play.

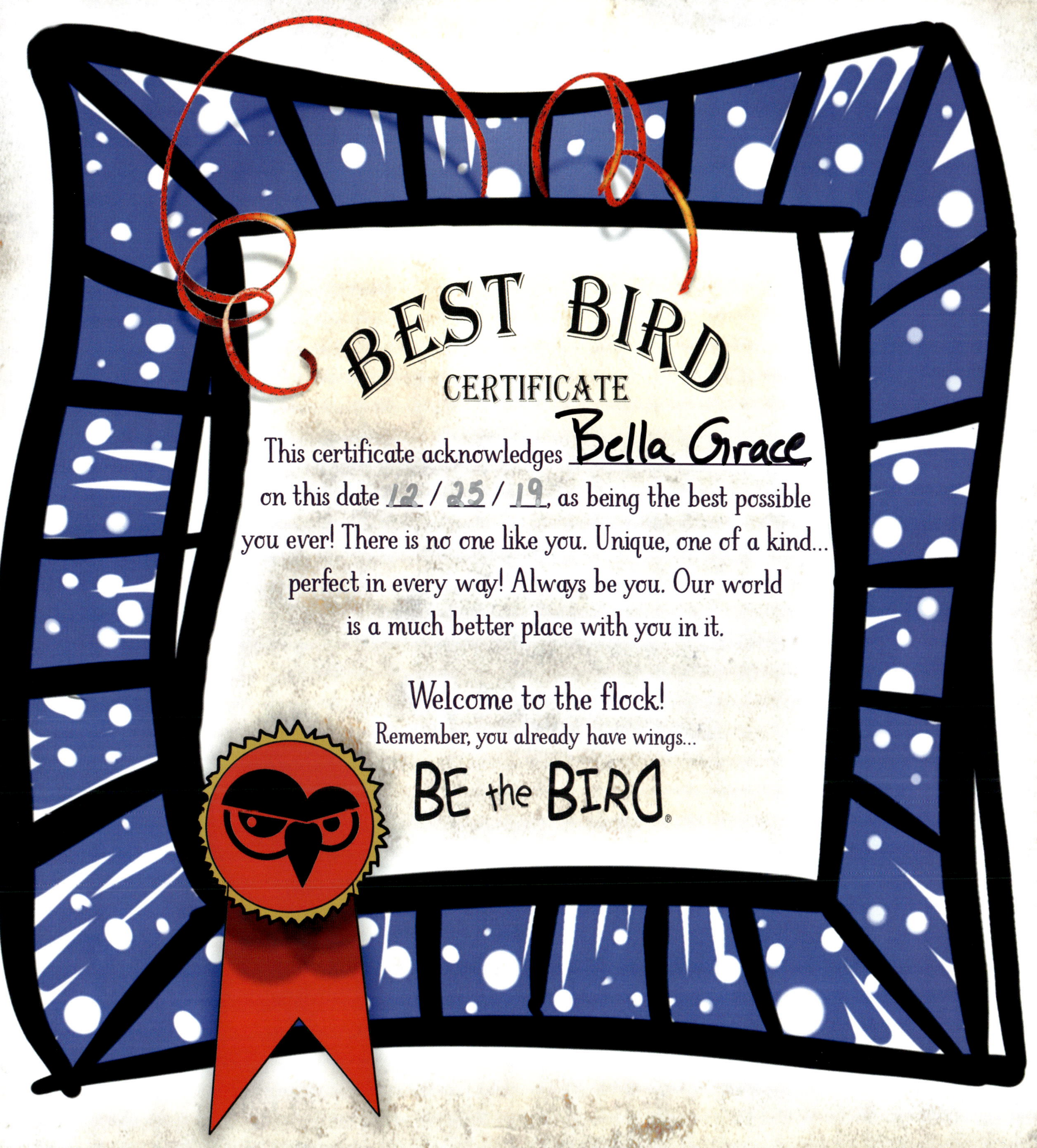
BEST BIRD
CERTIFICATE
This certificate acknowledges Bella Grace,
on this date 12 / 25 / 19, as being the best possible
you ever! There is no one like you. Unique, one of a kind...
perfect in every way! Always be you. Our world
is a much better place with you in it.
Welcome to the flock!
Remember, you already have wings...
BE the BIRD®

Illustrations by Richard Lorenz
Story by Tina Louise


Published by Silent Echoes Studio.



Library of Congress Control Number: 2019945667
Be the Bird, Book 1 / Illustrated by Richard Lorenz / Story by Tina Louise
ISBN: 978-0-9834235-0-8

Printed in the United States of America by
Signature Book Printing
First Edition September 2019
Book design by Surrogate Press®

www.silentechoesstudio.com
www.bethebird.com

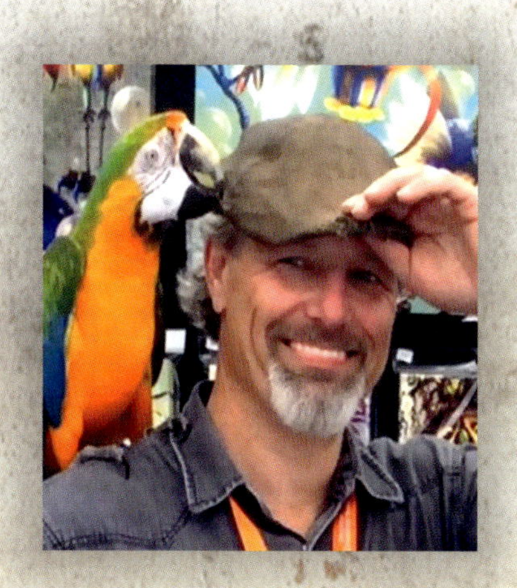

**RICHARD LORENZ** – German born, Louisiana artist and creator of the popular series – **'Be the Bird'.®** A professional artist for the past 30 years, Richard has made a career from his art, with many prestigious awards and accolades in this industry. Painting in oils, acrylics, and now digital, his work has a timeless message for young people (of all ages). Richard's work can be found in exhibitions, galleries, and private collections worldwide.

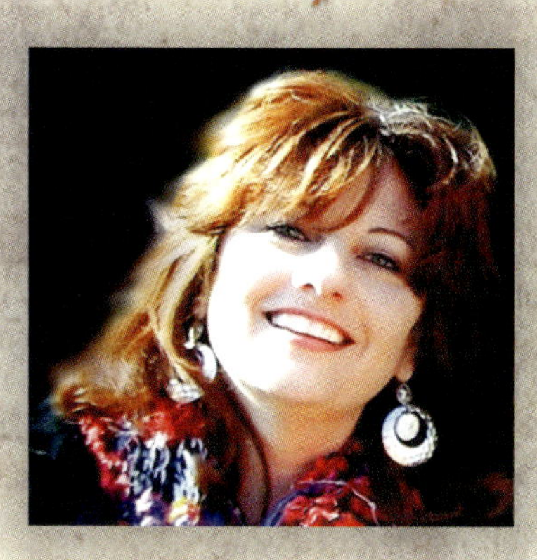

**TINA LOUISE** – Author and photographer from Cloutierville, Louisiana. For the past 30 years, Tina has made a career from her passion as a freelance writer, newspaper editor, award winning author and photographer. Her many accolades include: Lagniappe Magazine, Acadiana Profile, Sunshine Artist Magazine as well as her numerous contributions to the Associates Press. She is also the creator and instigator of the original **'Southern Dusty Angels'.™**

Together, Rick and Tina have 5 children and maintain – Silent Echoes Studio® – a publishing company for all of their creations. They continue to be inspired each and every day as their 6 grandchildren find their wings and discover the magic found within.

www.BetheBird.com  www.SilentEchoesStudio.com

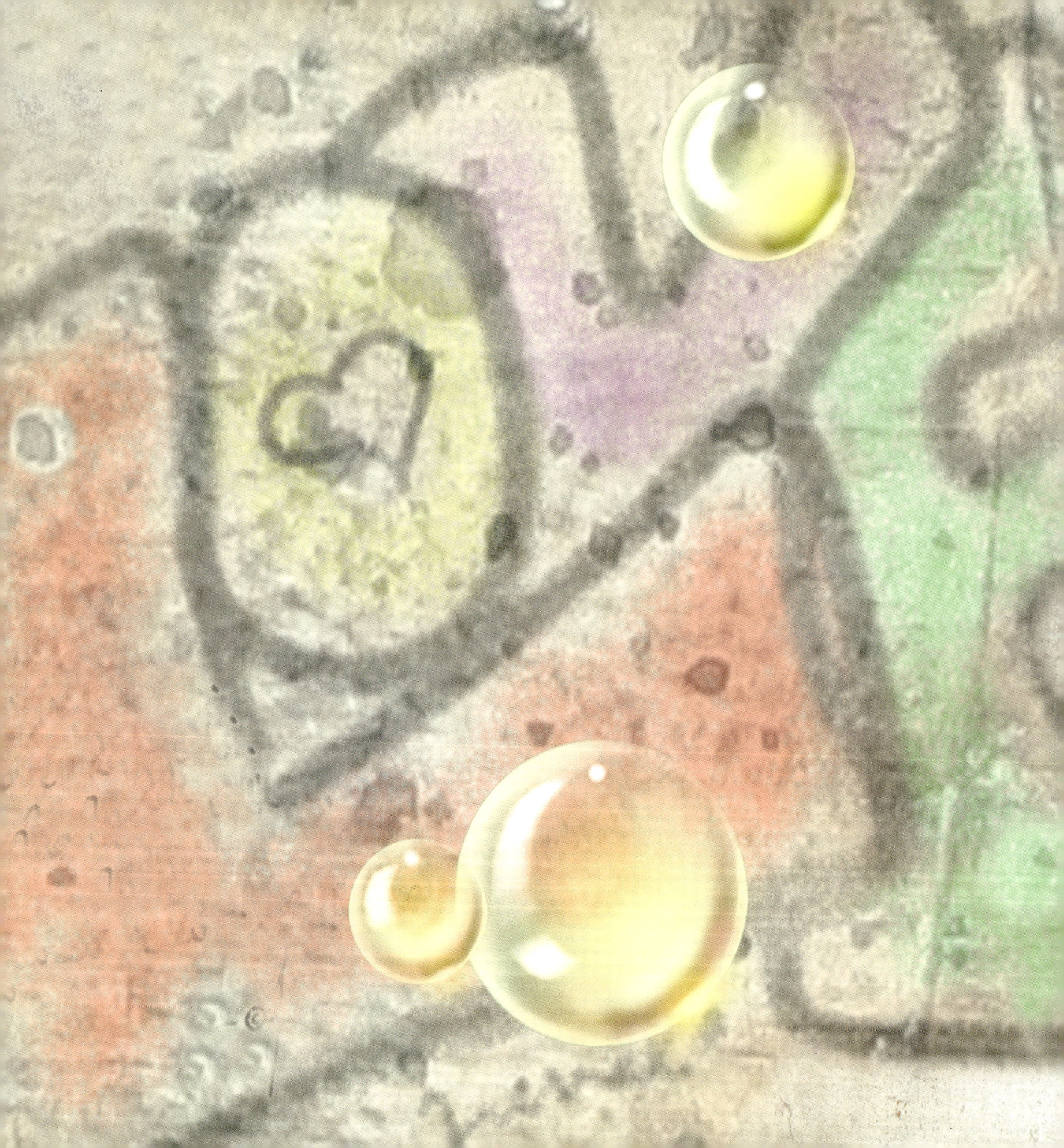

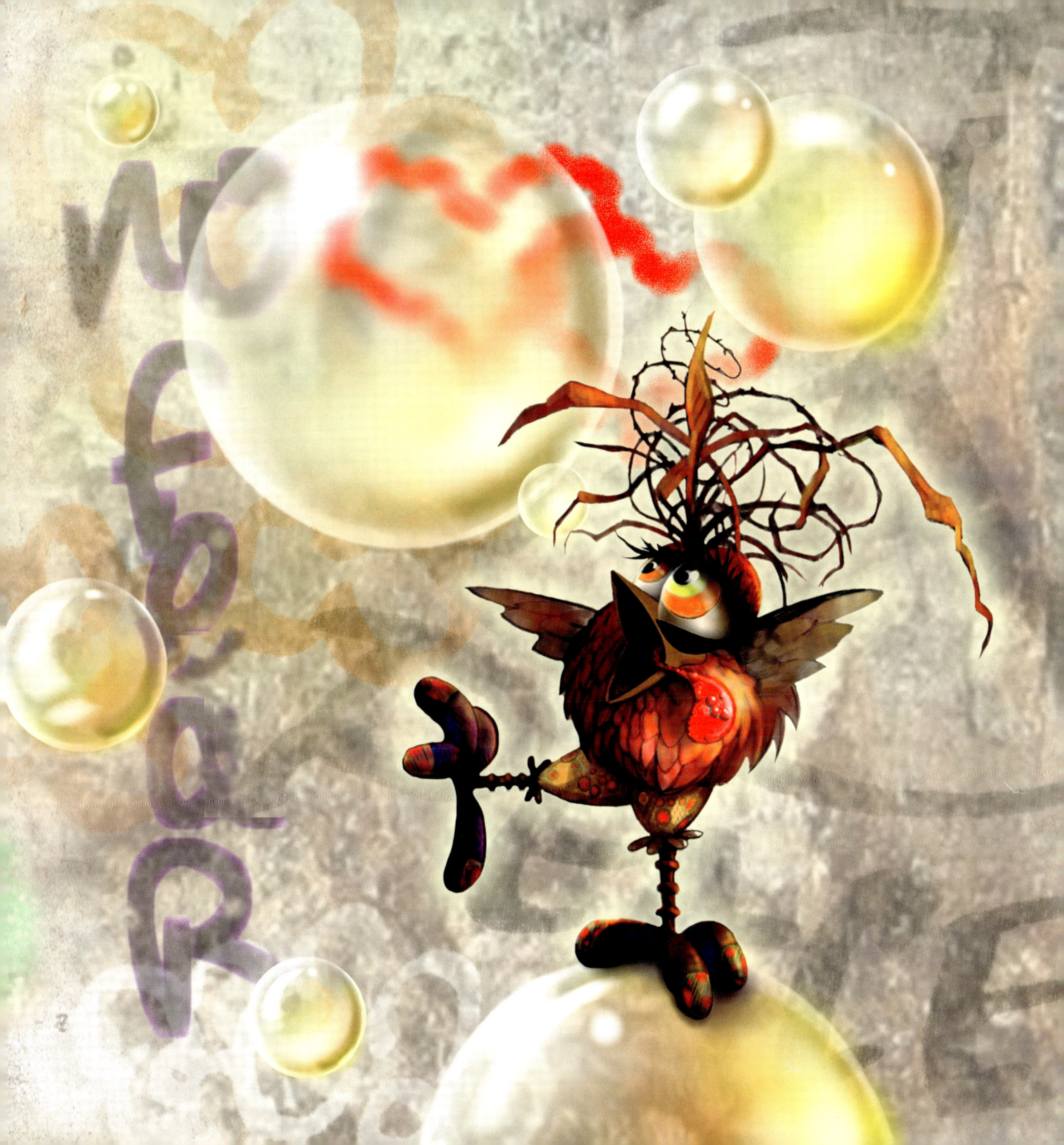